Dear Jim.

Spotted just a couple of
things that you may
like to include. - Think you
have done a good job!!
Tell you of the things I
read when you next phone.

Love Diana

Dear Tom,

Spotted just a couple of
things that you used
the if evaluate. — Think you
have done a good job :)

Tell you of the things I
read when you next phone.

love Diana

Remembering The People of Bramcote

How one village was affected by World War One

Bramcote History Group 2010

BRAMCOTE
HISTORY GROUP

First published in 2010 by Bramcote History Group.

Printed by the Russell Press, Russell House, Bulwell Lane, Basford, Nottingham NG6 OBT.

ISBN:978-0-9566434-0-7

This book was published with the assistance of:
Nottingham Community Federation, Grassroots Grants.

Front cover designed by Janet Martin and based on an original photograph of Bramcote in 1907. Picture courtesy of Reflections of a Bygone Age, Keyworth.

CONTENTS

Foreword

No shots were fired in Bramcote between 1914 and 1918 yet the people living here in those years, like their counterparts in thousands of other communities, were changed enormously by World War One.

A bronze tablet in the parish church bearing a simple list of names and a village hall are the only visual reminders of a time that residents must have wished both to forget yet remember.

Bramcote History Group decided to undertake research into how The Great War was experienced by our village. This is not a military history focusing on each serving man's war record --- it is an attempt to "paint a picture" of both community life and individuals' experiences immediately before, during and after the conflict.

Long may we remember their fortitude.

We would like this book and our gift of a cabinet to be utilised in Bramcote Memorial Hall, for displays relating to this era of our village's history, to make our remembrance more meaningful and also to encourage people to contribute further to the history group's archives.

We are very grateful to all those who have undertaken research and particularly to those who have shared their families' memories with us.

Bramcote History Group acknowledges, with thanks, the generous financial donation from Nottinghamshire Community Foundation, Grassroots Grants.

Bramcote Village in 1914

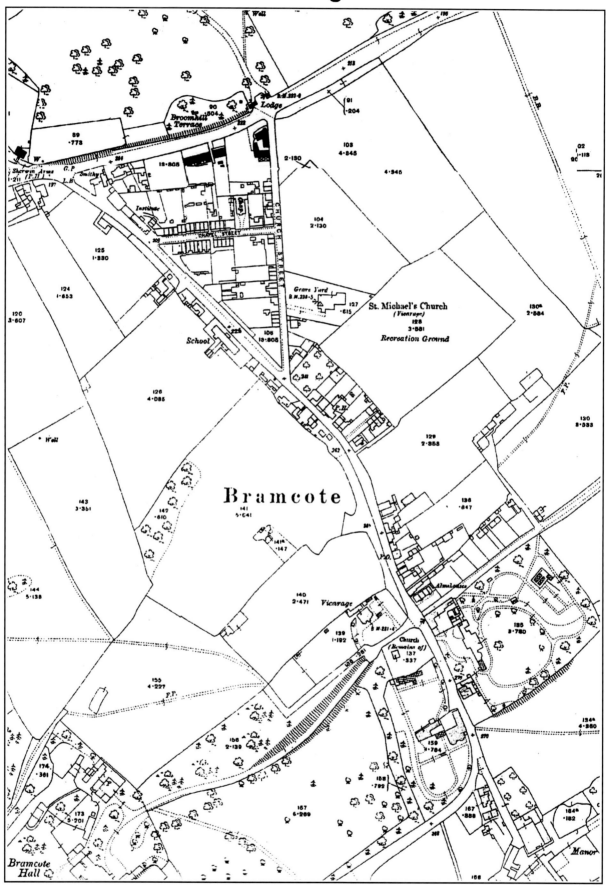

Extract from Ordnance Survey Map for Bramcote:
sheet no. : XLI.II, published 1914

2

Bramcote - Pre-War
A bustling village, little anticipating The Great War

"Bramcote is a village, pleasantly seated on lofty hills, 2 miles west from Beeston station and five miles west by south from Nottingham. The area of the village is 1,064 acres with the chief crops being wheat, barley, oats, beans and roots. The moor is a hamlet, half a mile north." This is a description of the village in Kelly's Directory of 1912 and the Census of 1911 tells us there were 683 people living here in 156 separate households.

This rather formal description, however, tells little about the community itself. It was a busy, self-sufficient village where folk would have known about one another's good and bad news as they congregated at the shops and went about their day to day business. Whilst there were some wealthy residents, most of the villagers would have had little to spare but they seem to have enjoyed social events whenever an opportunity presented itself.

The Coronation of King George V and Queen Mary had been a cause for much celebration according to The Ilkeston Pioneer of 23rd June 1911. There had been a procession throughout the village followed by a church service and a tea for every child in the parish at 3pm, a meat tea for unmarried adults at 4pm and finally a third tea for the married folk. It was clearly an orderly village! Later, however, there were three-legged races, climbing the greasy pole, a bonfire and fireworks and on the following morning cock crowing and egg laying competitions.

Church Street, Bramcote 1907
Picture courtesy of Reflections of a Bygone Age, Keyworth

Many events in the village were centred on the Church of St. Michael and All Angels where the minister from 1900 onwards was The Reverend A. E. Hughes. Not least of these was the Jubilee Service for the Church in March 1911. The Bishop of Southwell spoke on this occasion about the importance of the Sunday school work and the need to instil strict moral codes into the children of the village. A church magazine, serving

Bramcote cum Attenborough was begun in 1912 with a monthly copy costing 1d. There was also a well-attended United Methodist Chapel though it was not licensed for marriages until 1930.

The Public Elementary School on Town Street could accommodate 160 boys and girls, up to 14 years of age. In 1912 the average attendance, for reasons we can only speculate on, though there had been many cases of measles in the village the year before, was only 101. The headmaster was Harry Sutton but great interest was taken in the education of the young by Mrs. F. C. Smith of Bramcote Hall who awarded yearly prizes at both the day and the Sunday schools.

Church and school came together in May 1912 when about 40 children were provided with a daily soup dinner at the school to help those whose fathers were out of work. The headmaster and his wife, Mr. and Mrs. Sutton, personally donated 60 loaves of bread. During the summer holidays of 1913 the school, which had been built in 1885, was "undergoing needful painting and redecoration", according to the church magazine.

An institution that has disappeared but was important in pre-war Bramcote was the Parish Council which met regularly, with councillors being elected for three year terms. In1913. Major Holden had been appointed chairman and the other councillors were:

Frank Henson, *joiner*	Joseph Hewitt, *collier*
Benjamin Youell, *coachman*	John Husbands, *labourer*
George Jackson, *lace designer*	Naaman Turton, *miner*
John Mellor, *blacksmith*	Jesse Tomlinson, *miner*
Joseph Daykin, *miner*	Joseph Unsworth, *miner*

At the council meeting held in April 1914 improvements to the playground were discussed and Major Holden promised to provide two footballs for the boys. A complaint from Mrs. Husbands about the nuisance caused by the emptying of the pail closets was also considered!

Much of Bramcote was owned by the Holden family. Their family seat, Bramcote Hills House, was rented out to Ernest Wentworth Claye, a railway rolling stock manufacturer, in 1911 whilst Major Ernest Frank Holden was resident at The Grove but he did move into The Hills during the war years. Bramcote Hall was occupied by Mrs. Harriet Matilda Smith, the widow of Banker Smith, until her death on the 9th August 1914. The sudden death in 1913 of Henry Pearson in Egypt, where he had gone to improve his health left Laura Kate Pearson in The White House with three sons and two daughters. Henry, along with his brother Sir Louis Pearson, had established The Beeston Foundry Company, later to be known as Beeston Boiler Company. The Grange was occupied by Henry Houghton Enfield, the President of Nottingham Law Society in 1913, and three of his sisters.

Many villagers would have been employed in these houses as servants, ranging in status from kitchen maids to footmen and butlers, though several such positions would have been held by newcomers into the community. Others mainly earned their livings as miners, lace workers or agricultural workers. The miners would have worked at the Trowell and Wollaton pits and the lace workers at factories in Stapleford, Sandiacre, or Beeston.

A 1912 directory records the businesses in the village itself. There were 5 farmers: Elias Joule, Arthur Knapp, Richard Wells, Henry and William Willoughby and a market gardener, George Willoughby. Francis Burdett Eatch was the butcher; Tom Cope was the coal dealer, Miss Mary Turner the dressmaker and the Post Office/shop was run by Miss Margaret Broomhead. Other shopkeepers were: Thomas Ward, David Wilson and Cecil Moult who was also a beer retailer. The licensees were Charles Smith at The White Lion and Nathan Woodward at The Sherwin Arms.

Travel would have been mainly on foot but there were carriers to North Street, Nottingham every day and John Ginever was also working as a cab proprietor and advertising" brakes and wagonettes for pleasure parties".

There was a district nurse with Nurse Noble being succeeded by Nurse Atthill, who was based at Bankfield House, in 1913. Two bath chairs were kept for the use of the parish, one at the vicarage and one at Chilwell Hall, but they could only be borrowed and returned on the same day.

Whilst many social groups and activities revolved around the churches, such as The Band of Hope, the Temperance Society, the clothing club and sales of work held in a tent at the vicarage, there were some livelier activities. Mr. A. W. Dowson had created a Health and Strength Club for the men of the village, The Chilwell District Boy Scouts Company, led by Frederic Billows, had been started in 1911 and was attracting good numbers and organising summer camps in Skegness. The Misses Enfield decided the girls should not be left out and established a girls' club in 1912!

The Health and Strength Club

Thus we have a picture of a close community working hard and enjoying their limited leisure time whilst the storm clouds pressed nearer. Ominously, the church magazine noted that the presence of the camp of Sherwood Foresters had drawn large crowds to Chilwell Park.

The War Years

Life in Bramcote

1914 – 1918

1914 – The Call to Arms

Significant events on the war front

4th August Britain declared war on Germany

8th August Britain declared war on Austria

23rd August Retreat from Mons

18th October 1st Battle of Ypres

The Beeston Gazette and Echo of 15th August reported the text of the announcement of war:-

"Owing to the summary rejection by the German Government of the request by His Majesty's Government for assurance that the neutrality of Belgium would be respected, His Majesty's Government has declared to the Germans that a state of war exists between Great Britain and Germany from 11pm on 4th August".

Lord Kitchener, the War Minister, had begun his recruiting campaign on 7th August, calling for men aged between 19 and 30 to join the British Army and many were keen to do so with large numbers enlisting. Within a month Kitchener had raised the recruiting age limit to 35 and by the middle of September 500,000 had volunteered their services.

Initially these men had a choice of the regiment and unit they were attached to, though obviously this changed as the war progressed and men were simply drafted into regiments which suffered great losses.

Locally, men rushed to the Derby Barracks and before many days had elapsed, a recruitment office was opened in Ilkeston at the headquarters of the 5th Battalion Sherwood Foresters (Territorial) on Stanton Road. Eventually other recruitment centres were set up across the county.

Lord Kitchener wants you

After the form filling and the examinations, the process concluded by the recruit 'taking the King's Shilling' and the recruiting sergeant taking his sixpence per man. The recruit then went home, receiving his joining instructions and travel warrant a day or two later.

Generally, men joined up because they believed it was their patriotic duty. Some did so because their mates had enlisted and invariably they would join the same regiment. Others felt pressure from their families to volunteer. A few might have seen it as the chance for a brief holiday with pay. The war was expected to be over by Christmas.

News of a local and very early casualty must have been quite a shock for Bramcote folk. Harry Brocklesby Bartram had married Alice Eugenia Smith, daughter of Frederic 'Banker' Smith of Bramcote Hall. A handsome figure in his cavalry uniform it would have been hard for people to understand how he could have succumbed in one of the first confrontations of the war and died within days of reaching home.

Certainly the anxiety of the families of the Bramcote men listed as serving by mid December 1914 must have been heightened by this early death. The Ilkeston Pioneer printed a roll of honour of men serving with the colours in mid December so we can see who the early enlisters from Bramcote were:-

Claude Chappell, *Chapel Street*
Leonard Chappell, *Chapel Street*
Albert Clarke, *recorded as living on both*
                 Chapel Street and Town Street
Charles Geoffrey Claye, *Bramcote Hills House*
Harold Cooke, *Town Street*
John Thomas Cope, *Church Street*
Joseph Edwards, *Church Street*
Bernard Mellor, *The Forge*
James Mellows, *Town Street*
Noel Gervis Pearson, *The White House, Town Street*
Harry Swift, *Town Street*

Captain Harry Bartram

These men were from a complete cross section of the community with very different ages and status. Claude Chappell was just 16 whilst Harry Swift was 35 years of age. Some like Joseph Edwards were labourers or like John Cope working in the mines whilst Charles Claye and Noel Pearson came from affluent backgrounds. Bernard Mellor, working in his father's smithy, would have been struggling for work as horses were commandeered for the front and he would have enlisted to gain an income.

Thus the exodus of the young and fit men began and those who were left, often much older, found themselves taking on roles that they had previously retired from. They could not have guessed at the end of 1914 for how long the temporary measures would last.

The Smithy at Bramcote,
on the corner of Derby Road and Town Street

Bramcote Hall

Harry Bartram was the only man with local connections to lose his life in the first year of the conflict but his wife's family, the Smiths, had to endure two funerals that year. Bramcote Hall, positioned behind the old church tower at the top of Moss Drive was probably the biggest property in the village and Mrs. Harriet Matilda Smith, the widow of Frederic Chatfield Smith, who lived there, was the richest lady in Bramcote. She appears to have been a popular person and she was certainly a generous benefactor in the community. She died on 9th August, just after war had been declared, from "exhaustion" according to her death certificate after rather a long illness.

Harriet Smith

The grave at St. Michael's Church, Bramcote

The funeral that ensued was reported in The Nottingham Guardian with the comment that "It was not surprising to see so numerous an attendance"......because she was "held in affectionate esteem by everyone who knew her". Thirty members of the Constabulary lined the path to the church and a troop of Boy Scouts lined the entrance and representatives of many city and county charities and organisations were in attendance.

Images of Sherwood Foresters marching in Lenton c.1914 - courtesy of Nottingham City Council and www.picturethepast.org.uk

1915 – Eager Enlistment?

Significant events on the war front
22nd April to 25th May 2nd Battle of Ypres
25th September to 8th October Battle of Loos

WW1 Recruitment propaganda message on
The Exchange Building (forerunner of The Council House)
Courtesy of Nottingham City Council and www.picturethepast.org.uk

This was the year when Bramcote women and children really began to lose their menfolk. The military records show that enlistment of Bramcote men was at its height in 1915 and height itself became an issue for the Sherwood Foresters. In February of 1915 they began to recruit for a "bantam battalion" in which men of lesser stature (i.e. 5 ft to 5 ft 3 ins.) could serve.

Those who had not volunteered by the autumn must have felt very pressurised as a special meeting of the Parish Council was held in the schoolroom on Tuesday 9th November at 7pm to make arrangements for a recruiting canvass. Five members were present and Major Holden took the Chair. A review of men who had not enlisted from Bramcote took place and canvassers were chosen to encourage 32 specific men to serve their country at the front. The canvassers were Major E.F. and Mrs. Holden, George Arthur Jackson and Peter Henry Burton.

Kitchener's Army

SHERWOOD FORESTERS
Bantam Battalion

RECRUITING
HAS NOW COMMENCED
at the
MECHANICS HALL, NOTTINGHAM
And all Recruiting Stations in the counties of
Lincolnshire, Leicestershire, Staffordshire,
Derbyshire and Nottinghamshire between the
hours of 9 am – 6.30 pm

MEASUREMENT STANDARD
HEIGHT: Minimum 5 ft to 5 ft 3 ins

Married men should produce marriage certificates
and birth certificates of children. Men can be
immediately medically examined and attested at any
Recruiting Station. If passed they will be given Railway
Warrant to the Headquarters at Nottingham.

JOIN AT ONCE

BANTAMS
Did you ever see a Bantam in a fight?
No other bird can "stick it"
Like a Bantam, or can "lick it"
And you never saw a Bantam taking fright.

(From a new song by Stephen West
music by Edward Watson)

GOD SAVE THE KING

Bantams wanted

There is no record of who the 32 men were or how they reacted to these canvassers but they must have felt intimidated and some would surely have capitulated to the pressure.

An article in the Beeston Gazette and Echo of 21st August 1915 also reflected how public opinion was changing. Mr. Stephen Hetley Pearson, of The White House, Bramcote, who was the founder of the Beeston Boys' Brigade, was offering a golden sovereign for every stripe gained by any of the boys who had enlisted. Yet a year previously, again in the Beeston Gazette of 29th August 1914, Mr. Pearson had been at pains to disassociate the Boys' Brigade from organisations such as the Scouts who had offered their services to the government for war-like duties. He said at that time, "We do not wish any of our members' parents to think that we have fostered a fighting spirit in their lads". Patriotism was now in the ascendancy and by the end of the war many of the lads had been buried in foreign soil.

Stephen Hetley Pearson

In Bramcote the reality of what the serving men were facing at the front was still vague as the only village fatality of 1915 was Gunner Albert Thorpe who died in Newcastle hospital from disease on 19th March before he was due to depart for service abroad. Civilians at home were becoming more concerned though about the plight of those abroad. At a Parish Council meeting on 7th July, a letter with reference to the Belgian Relief Fund was read and the council unanimously expressed their sympathy and their willingness to do whatever was in their power.

The press began to suggest ways in which those left at home could be more practically supportive of the troops. The Beeston Gazette and Echo of 9th January printed a pattern for the "best soldier's scarf".

BEST SOLDIER'S SCARF.

DOUBLE AND CAN BE USED AS A HELMET.

We give below the method for a double knitted scarf, which is one of the most ideal "comforts" it is possible for the soldier to possess. If loosely knitted it is beautifully soft and warm. One end can be tucked in and slipped over the head like a cap, while the other end is wound round the neck.

It is an immense advantage to reduce the soldier's kit and make it as light as possible, and this muffler does away with the necessity of a helmet in addition to a scarf.

It is most important in following the method to use the right kind of wool, a really good soft quality. The lady who made this particular scarf describes the task as being "as easy as falling off a log," though we must confess ourselves that we feel she should have added "to an experienced knitter." It is a consolation to hear that another lady who has tried the method found it very difficult at first, but very soon became accustomed to the stitch.

Materials Required:—No. 7 needles 7ozs. (roughly)of 5-ply super fingering.

Cast on 76 stitches. *Slip one purlwise, take wool to back, knit one, bring wool forward and repeat from*

The scarf must be knitted loosely and should be ten inches wide and two yards long when finished. In casting off knit two stitches together or the end will be full. If worked by a tight knitter extra stitches should be cast on.

Care should be taken not to make a mistake or the sides will be caught together.

On 19th July there would probably have been much local interest at the auction of "The Stud Farm, Bramcote". It would appear that this had been run by Mr. Herbert Copeland, a butcher, in buildings at the rear of The Sherwin Arms. The property itself was not for sale as that was part of the Holden estate which was eventually sold in 1919. On this occasion animals, farming and agricultural machinery, saddlery and stable equipment, hay and manure along with some household furniture were offered in various lots. Presumably Mr. Copeland had had to give up his business because of the requisition of horses for war work.

Horse sale at Ilkeston in 1914
Courtesy of Derbyshire Local Studies Libraries and www. picturethepast.org.uk

There was a rather sad spectacle at the end of the year as the three unmarried daughters of the late Frederic and Harriet Smith, Katherine Maud, Ethel and Cicely, left Bramcote Hall to live at Blidworth Dale. Letters printed in the church magazine indicate that this was a very hard time for them for they were leaving their family home when the eldest sister, Katherine Maud, was clearly unwell. Presumably they lacked the income to continue to run such a large property and household staff.

The Reverend A. E. Hughes' letter to the Smith sisters
included the following:

> "The villagers of Bramcote......ask you to accept and hope you find useful the afternoon tea tray and cake stand..... and bed-coverlet for Miss Smith, whose removal in her illness they feel to be unspeakably sad......very little token of their deep and loving sympathy and of their grateful recollection of your earnest work on their behalf in bygone years."

All the Smith daughters had served as Sunday school teachers and Ethel Smith was also given a pencil case by her young charges.

This marked the end of the influential, generous and well-respected Smith family's residence in Bramcote.

The three Smith sisters : Katherine Maud, Ethel and Cicely, as a child.

Blidworth Dale
Photograph courtesy of Blidworth and District History and Heritage Society

1916 – Conscription and Zeppelin raids

Significant events on the war front
21st February to 18th December Battle of Verdun
1st July to 17th November Battle of The Somme

From the beginning of this year, it became abundantly clear that more and more men were needed at the front and there would be very few who would be able to avoid conscription. On 27th January 1916 the government introduced the Military Service Act which specified that men aged from 18 to 41 were liable to be called up for service unless they were married or widowed with children or served in a reserved profession, usually industrial, but which also included clergymen. This was swiftly deemed insufficient because a revision was made on the 25th May which meant all men aged 18 to 41, regardless of their marital status, could be required to serve. Those who had previously been declared unfit could be re-examined and time-expired servicemen could have their service extended.

The vicar, The Reverend A. E. Hughes, writing in the church magazine, called upon everyone to contribute to the cause. He said,

"Many are fighting for their country......many are dying for their country....what are we doing for her?" He asked the parish to pray and requested that the services be marked by *"large congregations and intense earnestness".* A list of all the soldiers currently serving from Attenborough, Bramcote, Chilwell and Toton was printed in this magazine under the heading "Soldiers' Prayer List". The names of 52 men from Bramcote are recorded there and, in a small village, we can surmise that each one of them would have been known by most of the residents and duly prayed for.

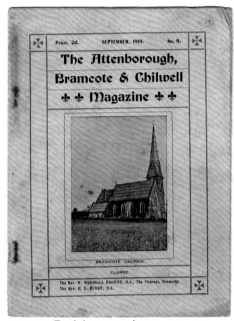

Parish magazine cover

It must have seemed as though the war was coming closer to home as Zeppelin raids were reported in the local press. The Beeston Gazette dated 5th February said:

"The Zeppelin raid on Monday night (31st January) is now seen to have been the biggest of the kind that has so far been made. First we are allowed to know that six or seven airships took part in the invasion and that they got as far as the Midland counties........The raiders were, it appears, hampered by a thick fog ...... the casualties are given as 54 killed and 67 injured .... a not inconsiderable butcher's bill for the enemy's maiden venture into the heart of England." The press was banned from releasing the precise localities that were attacked but the evidence was often there for all to see.

Zeppelin raid at Castle Gate
Courtesy of Nottingham City Council and www.picturethepast.org.uk

Clara Mowbray, who had been born in 1907, was living in Courtyard off Cow Lane at this time and she would recount in later life how she nearly received an early birthday present because of the Zeppelins. A few days before her birthday, which was 2nd February, the air was filled with the dreadful, droning noise of the engines as a gigantic Zeppelin moved slowly overhead. Her mother pulled her beneath the kitchen table and, in fear as well as to distract the girl, asked her small daughter if she would like her birthday present then and there! Clara very bravely said she would wait and the Zeppelin passed by, fortunately without any harm being inflicted, but she never forgot the incident.

Charles Lavelle also mentioned the Zeppelin raids when he wrote, from his base with the Sherwood Foresters in Sunderland, to his friend Stanley Briggs in Bramcote, "I hear you got the Zeppelins rather close on Monday night. (31st January) I hope they won't start that route very often".

Clara Mowbray on her engagement day

By mid March however there was a victim in Beeston: William Henry Thurman of Wilkinson Avenue had fallen backwards and died within minutes from the rupture of an aneurysm but independent witnesses blamed this indirectly on the Zeppelin raid that had taken place.

Uncertainty seems to have been prevalent in many areas of local life in 1916. People would have realised that the war was not going well if more and more men were being called up. There would have been fear of a long term bombardment from the Zeppelins and notions of a swift conflict would have been dispensed with. Should they try to maintain normal traditions within the village? At the beginning of the year the vicar had suggested that it would be "better this year to forgo the usual teas which at other times are so happy and profitable".

There was a need for another replacement on the Bramcote Parish Council too. Much sorrow had been expressed in October 1915 when Benjamin Youell, coachman to "Banker" Smith and a resident at Bramcote Hall, had died. The person elected, Nathan Woodward, was soon in trouble with his fellow council members, however, because his donkey had been feasting in the allotments!

Mr. and Mrs. Benjamin Youell

As 1916 drew to a close and people reflected on the events of the year, many of them must have been downhearted. Four Bramcote men had died on the Somme and it is hard to imagine what the effect might have been on the village as the news was relayed. George Cooke and Charles Lavelle had died within two days of one another in July and Harry Tomlinson and Ernest Eatch's deaths followed in the autumn. There were no funerals for these men whereas the funeral of Katherine Maud Smith on 18th December at Bramcote would have been well attended. When she had left Bramcote for Blidworth, along with her sisters, she had been in frail health so her demise, though very sad, was not unexpected. Bramcote's young soldiers, however, had left the village in good spirits and perfect health.

Most activities actually continued as usual with jumble sales, and meetings of the Band of Hope and the Women's Total Abstinence Group being regular occurrences. Mothers with babies under 12 months old were invited to Chilwell Hall on the first Thursday of each month at 2.30pm with Mrs. Allen, the wife of Judge Wilfred Baugh Allen of Southfields House, Common Lane providing a taxi service from the top of Cow Lane at 2pm. By March too the vicar had relented and gave an invitation for all unmarried young women aged 14 to 35 in the village to attend a tea in the school. A collection for motor ambulances for the front, undertaken by some Bramcote ladies, resulted in £6 14s 6d being raised.

There were changes at the vicarage during the year as The Reverend Hughes left the parish on 30th April 1916 to be replaced, exactly two months later, by The Reverend Walter Marshall Browne who had previously been serving as the curate at St. Ann's in Nottingham. He was to become a very important figure in the village as he was an energetic man who seemed to thrive on being actively involved in all parish matters.

The Reverend A. E. Hughes

The Reverend W. M. Browne
in later life

The Vicarage, Bramcote

1917 Austerity sets in

Significant events on the war front

7th June to 10th November 3rd Battle of Ypres

"We are living among such big events, that we can none of us measure how great or how rapid is the change from life as we knew it three years ago.......the progress towards victory is much slower than we hoped at first". So wrote The Reverend Walter Marshall Browne in his monthly address for January 1917. Interestingly he also speculated about the huge changes that might take place at the end of the conflict, envisaging lots of new legislation with the railways, shipping, mining and labour all being nationalised.

For now economising was at the forefront of people's thoughts along with devising further practical ways in which people in the village could help those at the front. The Bramcote War Savings Association had been set up at the very end of 1916 and in January 1917 there were 32 members, with Harry Sutton, the headmaster, taking on the role of treasurer. The Bramcote Comforts Fund had collected £17 1s 0d at the end of January and those who had recently left school, taken up employment and were still living at home were particularly encouraged to make donations. The children in the village were learning a little of the effects of the war too as a decision was taken not to award Sunday school prizes this year.

Whilst Bramcote men were fighting abroad, there were also serving soldiers based in Bramcote. Fourteen were billeted at Ivy House on Church Street with Tom and Lizzie Watson and their daughter Elsie Abbott recalled one very large bedroom with seven double beds in it for the soldiers! These men were manning an anti-aircraft gun site on the top of Bluebell Hill off Common Lane. It was decided in February 1917 that the schoolroom should be opened each evening from 7 until 10p.m. as a social room for the soldiers and villagers provided games, papers and magazines for their amusement.

Ivy House, at the corner of Church Street and Derby Road

Perhaps some thought was given to the soldiers being further employed as agricultural workers and crop guardians during 1917.

The Nottinghamshire War Agricultural Committee was enquiring in January about the probable quantity of seed potatoes that would be required in the village. A special meeting was convened on 8th February to consider this matter. The Clerk of the Parish Council was instructed to speak to individual cottagers about their requirements and Mr. Woodward offered to store the seed potatoes but could not undertake to weigh them out. There was another special meeting at the end of March to arrange the distribution of the potatoes and consideration was given to the replacement of wire netting and stakes in the allotments, but the latter was considered too costly. On 11th June a decision was made to purchase a potato sprayer at a cost of £3, along with two boxes of chemicals at a cost of £1 4s 0d, but a month later "the Clerk was instructed to telegraph the Food Production Department asking that the sprayer be forwarded without delay as the matter was urgent."

Following an announcement in the House of Commons on 16th April 1917 that the loss of food owing to the depredations of sparrows was so serious that the Board of Agriculture had urged the formation of sparrow clubs throughout the country, Bramcote responded. The Parish Council decided in May of 1917 that a Sparrow Club should be formed for the parish, with the council giving one pound towards expenses and Major Holden promising to match that donation personally. It was agreed that "Mr. Mellor be Treasurer and that he receive, pay for, and destroy the tails and heads". It was agreed further that Mr. Burton should solicit subscriptions from the farmers in the parish and that the scoutmaster should be approached with a view to obtaining the assistance of the boy scouts. Unfortunately there are no accounts of how effective the sparrow campaign was and we have been unable to find any local recipes for sparrow pie so we are left to speculate as to whether the birds brought variety to the dinner table.

A Bramcote Boy Scout,
Charles Clifford

Bramcote's housewives had to be particularly economical with food and the vicar urged everyone to keep within the voluntary ration of bread but there could still be jam with it. This recipe for jam appeared in the church magazine:

"A good jam may be made with
6 oz of sugar,
2½ teaspoonfuls of salt to each pound of fruit.
The salt taste will disappear after it has been kept six weeks".

Taste buds were being challenged in another direction too. A local dairy farmer was summoned to Shire Hall for selling milk which was "deficient in fat". It was decided that the milk had not been tampered with but the cow had to be disposed of and the magistrates warned the defendant to "exercise care in future and to keep only the best cows".

In these difficult times, thoughts didn't centre entirely on the day to day and practical matters though and there is evidence that folk were reflective and questioning about "the greater scheme of things". The churches were actively involved in community matters as well as providing places of solace. In February of 1917 a confirmation service was held at St. Michael's and 33 candidates were presented to the Bishop, 11 of them coming from Bramcote. Following the service the clergy and congregation proceeded to the new burial ground where the Bishop, standing outside the east wall of the church, consecrated the additional ground, in a solemn prayer. The land, amounting to about one acre, had been donated by Captain Ernest Frank Holden. Another gift for the church had been recently received from Harry Sutton, the headmaster of the school. He had given a brass cross for use on the communion table in memory of his late wife, Mary, who had also taught at the school.

In the autumn, the Vicar suggested to his parishioners that "now the evenings are drawing in, the knitting needles ought to be at work" and accounts show that some of the Comforts Fund savings were spent on wool purchased at Miss Broomhead's shop, which was also the Post Office, at the top of Town Street. Money was also spent on cigarettes and cards for the men. In December the plan was to send a parcel to the value of 3 shillings to all Bramcote men serving in the army and cigarettes were to be sent through the agency of the Football Post Fund.

The Post Office and shop run by Miss Broomhead on Town Street

There was much sadness at the end of the year as Wilf Headland was discharged injured to return home in October and in December, John Starbuck died from his wounds in Egypt. News of the death of Stephen Hetley Pearson on the Somme must have stunned people in Bramcote and further afield as he was well known in this area as the Captain of the 17th Nottingham (Beeston) Boys' Brigade. A memorial service took place at Beeston Parish Church for "Mr. Hetley". At Bramcote, permission was being sought to erect a permanent memorial within the church to one of the "glorious war dead" in the form of a marble tablet recording the death of Captain Harry Bartram, who had died in September 1914.

The Vicar's letter at the end of the year spoke of "the solace of old memories keeping us steadfast till the dawn of peace".

Bramcote Church of England School, Town Street, Bramcote

Harry and Mary Sutton with some pupils at Bramcote Church of England School.
Harry gave a brass cross to the church in 1917, in memory of his late wife, Mary.

1918 - The End in Sight

Significant events on the war front

21st March German Spring offensive began

25th April German offensive halted

1st August Allied offensive began

11th November Armistice signed

The year began with a major 'offensive' in the centre of Nottingham which was designed to raise revenue to "drive a nail into the Kaiser's coffin" according to the local press. People were being encouraged to visit the market place where one of the tanks, that were being displayed in various cities, would be on show. The idea was that attendees would also purchase war savings certificates at 15s 6d each. An executive committee was appointed in Beeston to work this national scheme at a more local level and in the parish magazine for March, every household was asked to purchase one certificate or war bond during the National War Savings Week from 4th to 9th March.

Today we would find it very easy to travel into Nottingham for a special event, such as viewing the tank, but transport was not so readily available in 1918. At the parish council meeting of 10th January it was agreed that a resolution should be forwarded to Stapleford Rural District Council stating that it was most desirable that improved communication with Nottingham should be afforded by the placing of a motor bus on the road between Stapleford and Nottingham. Kelly's Directory of 1925 recorded that "two series of motor omnibuses pass the Derby Road end of the village at frequent intervals from Nottingham to Stapleford and back" so the need for better transport was eventually recognised.

Nottingham Road, Stapleford with The Sherwin Arms on the left

Perhaps more pressing was the need to cultivate the land and grow as much food as possible. Dr. Goodwin, the Principal of Kingston Agricultural College was invited to deliver a lecture in the schoolroom on manures and manuring. He explained that soot could be helpful in encouraging leaf growth but "all that is black is not soot and it is as well not to buy unless you know that it is the genuine article". He also said that "the liquid part of farmyard manure should be kept so far as possible" along with lawn mowings, wood ashes and rotted vegetable matter as they all contain potash and "are therefore very valuable at the present time".

Perhaps this lecture led to the special meeting held on 9th April regarding the cutting up of the recreation ground into allotments. Mr. Enfield, who rented the grazing, had no objection so it was decided that a circular should be issued to villagers asking for applications for allotments to be sent in by 13th April. It was carried that the rent be 5 shillings for each allotment of 400 square yards. On 16th April another special meeting about the allotments took place and it was announced that there had been 10 applications from 8 persons. The records do not explain how the discussion then flowed but it was unanimously decided not to break up the recreation ground. An alternative plan was devised. The Bishop had apparently consented to the breaking up of the new part of the churchyard so the applicants were to be asked to accept an allotment there.

Henry Houghton Enfield

Behaviour in the churchyard was not always appropriate. Six unnamed boys were brought before the Parish Council in April charged with depredation in the old churchyard, presumably the burial ground adjacent to the tower on Town Street, and warned that a repetition would be followed by magisterial proceedings. All promised that it would not occur again.

Bramcote church tower with burial ground.

Whilst such incidents would undoubtedly have led to much local gossip or outrage, they were of little significance in comparison with the terrible local disaster that occurred on Monday 1st July. At 7.10pm a series of blasts from Chilwell Munitions Factory were heard throughout the area as nearly eight tons of explosive lifted itself skywards. 134 people were killed and 250 were injured. Clearly Bramcote folk would have been devastated by this tragedy and many must have lost friends and relatives who worked there though no Bramcote residents were listed amongst the dead. Herbert Hunt, who lived at Pinfold House on Church Street, was on his way home from work at the depot when the explosion occurred. One of his children, Stanley, had as usual, come out to meet him but Herbert sent Stanley home and went straight back to the depot to help.

Emma and Herbert Hunt of Pinfold House

The scenes he encountered must have been horrific but terms like "post traumatic stress disorder" did not exist in those times and we can only imagine how the rescuers, like the soldiers at the front, would have dealt with the carnage they had to witness.

It was in July that the vicar, The Reverend Walter Marshall Browne, embarked on his war service. He had sought permission previously from the Bishop to be released from office if he could be utilised in the services. He enlisted at Whitehall as a private in B Company of the Inns of Court Officer Training Corps. In a letter from Berkhampstead dated 28th July he wrote, "I am enjoying my life here very much and I would not have missed the experience for anything."

Mr. Dowson with Miss Mary Enfield in the foreground; the other ladies are unknown but could be her sisters.

He remained concerned about the village and suggested someone who might be a suitable candidate for the vacancy in the almshouses. He asked to be remembered to the Misses Enfield, Mr. Dowson and all the scouts. He also suggested that the men at the gun site still had some of the books from the village room and said he would be grateful if Mr. Dowson could ensure their return! The Enfield sisters and their brother lived at The Grange, Town Street, along with their cousin, Mr. Dowson.

The Grange, Town Street, courtesy of David Ottewell

1918 saw the armistice on 11th November but sadly it was also the year that witnessed most Bramcote casualties. In March three village men had died on almost consecutive days on The Somme: Frank Kirk dying on 21st, Richard Hallam dying on 22nd, and Arthur Burton dying on 24th of the month. In May Harry Swift died at Devonport and in July Charles Claye died in France. In September John Cope was discharged, returning home paralysed. Finally two lives were lost in Egypt towards the end of the year --- those of Richard Allen and John Pearson. The latter's death occurred at about the same time that the churchwardens were seeking permission to install a stained glass window at St. Michael's in memory of his twin brother, Stephen Hetley Pearson.

Whilst there must have been joy that the armistice had been signed, the village must also have been in a deep state of mourning at the loss of so many lives from such a small community.

The Immediate Post-War Years

Life in Bramcote

1919 – 1920

1919 - Change and celebrations

Evidence of a desire to mark the cessation of hostilities does not surface in Bramcote's records until the end of April when a special meeting was convened to consider in what way to celebrate the signing of the peace and also to discuss the question of a memorial to the war. It was proposed that there should be a celebration for the children and that £7 10s should be spent on flares and rockets. A committee, consisting of The Reverend Browne, Mr. Henson, Major Holden, Mr. Dowson and Mr. Woodward, was commissioned to carry out the project.

These initial thoughts gained momentum and by 12th May it had been determined through a vote at the parish meeting, with just one unnamed person dissenting, that the best way to commemorate the war was to erect an institute in which should be placed a list of the Bramcote men who had served their country, together with a list of those who had fallen. The committee to bring this to fruition was to consist of everyone on the Parish Council plus Mrs. Holden, Mrs. Pearson, Mrs. Birkin, Mrs. Adcock, Mrs. Chappell, Mrs. Browne, Miss Enfield, Mr. Daykin, Dr. and Mrs. Buckley, Mr. Towlson and Mr. Simpkin.

With this more serious and long term project underway, the simple party for the children was developed to such an extent that The Long Eaton Advertiser of 18th July announced that Bramcote would be celebrating the peace "in royal and befitting manner" the following weekend and gave considerable coverage to the events that took place in its reporting on 25th July, one week later. In turn we include a detailed report here as it conjures such delightful images:

"There have been many noteworthy weekends at Bramcote, but every previous record pales into insignificance before the remembrance of last week

The festivities began with a gorgeous fancy-dress ball on Friday night, and by special request the masquers promenaded the village prior to the dance, affording great satisfaction to the villagers. The sight was a splendid one, the various characters evoking much admiration.

Prizes had to be awarded for the best costumes, the judges being Mrs. Birkin, Mrs. Buckley and the Vicar, The Reverend. W. M. Browne. After a very careful consideration the awards were declared as follows: couple: Messrs. E. Simpkin and E. Eatch; lady: Miss N. Hunt; vote: Miss W. Headland; gentleman: Mr. W. Wrate (Beeston): vote: Mr. L. Daykin. (Presumably "vote" meant a prize awarded by the vote of the general public rather than by the judges.)

Of course it goes without saying that the dance was enjoyed. Miss M. E. Simpkin provided the music, and those who know Miss Simpkin's proficiency as a dance pianist, will know that nothing was lacking as far as the music was concerned. It was a galaxy of colour that ebbed and flowed with kaleidoscopic effect around the crowded ballroom and wholehearted enjoyment was the order of the evening.

Saturday dawned with excitement in the air. Especially were all the children agog, for this was their day!

At 1.30pm a large and picturesque procession formed at the old church, and marched through the village, preceded by the boy scouts and Band of the Comrades of the Great War from Nottingham. After a short service at the church they proceeded to the park, where sports and games occupied the time until tea was ready. Tea, in glorious plenty, was for everyone, young and old and there must have been very few indeed who did not enjoy themselves.

Oh! The cricket match. We must not forget the cricket match. The gentlemen played the ladies, these being twelve of the former and sixteen of the latter, although sad to say, ten of the ladies and seven of the gentlemen failed to score. Those who secured honours were as follows -

> *Ladies: Miss J. Hunt 7, Mrs. Elliott 4, N. Hunt 2, M. Jackson 1, G. Turton 1, Miss Osborne 1. Total: 16 with 14 extras. (The marital status of some of the ladies is not given in the report.)*

> *Gentlemen: J. Tomlinson 11, L. Daykin 11, S. Willoughby 5, C. Clifford 4, J. Daykin 2. Total: 33 with 3 extras.*

The gentlemen batted left-handed, with sticks, and also had to bowl left-handed, and there were some weird performances at times.

At the conclusion the gentlemen, who had won by six runs, presented the top scoring lady, Miss J. Hunt, with a box of chocolates. A collection was taken at the match for the War Memorial Fund.

More sports and plenty of prizes for the children followed, and then the dancing began, and the children looked forward to the fireworks. Then the rain began to come, and ultimately broke up the festivities, but even then everyone was completely satisfied that they had had a good time. Possibly the fireworks will be seen on Bank Holiday."

What a wonderful weekend this must have been. It is a pity that there are no photographs to accompany the written report. It does seem that fancy dress parades and competitions were popular events and we have uncovered and included here one picture of such an occasion that took place at around this time.

A photograph of some Bramcote men in fancy dress, taken in the school yard c1919 but not during the peace celebration weekend.

Another event during the summer that drew press attention was a Unionist Fete held in the grounds of Major Holden's property at Bramcote Hills on 4th July. It was attended by hundreds of people. Mr. Betterton, the M.P. for the division, gave a speech that was described as, "palpitating with imperial and patriotic fervour". He said that at no time was there "more need of a bold front to the insidious, mischief-making of pacifists and disguised Bolshevists, and every staunch Unionist must stand in the battle line as our brave lads have shown us how to do in France, Flanders and elsewhere". Following what was described as a "sumptuous tea" music was provided by a band of discharged soldiers and sailors. Later there was dancing until "darkness came on the scene and the tired merrymakers went home hoping that it would not be long ere there was such another event".

Bramcote Hills House

W. Stanley Briggs and Kathleen M. Lavelle who wed at St. Michael's Church in 1919

There were to be no further gatherings on this sort of scale through the autumn but it is clear that local people were wanting to hold social events and were enjoying the resumption of "normal" life again. In October a whist drive and dance, attracting about 120 dancers, was held in aid of funds for the cricket club. The harvest festival services, with one specifically for men, were well attended with offerings going to St. Dunstan's Home for blinded soldiers. The Sherwin Arms was the venue in late October for a gathering of demobbed soldiers who were treated by the cricket club to a supper and musical entertainment, in which some Bramcote veterans performed. In November there was a further social and dance in the schoolroom, perhaps in order to swell funds for the Memorial Hall, but marked particularly because of a presentation made to two popular young people, Stanley Briggs and Kathleen Lavelle, who were to marry at St. Michael's Church a few days later.

Aside from celebrations, there were two other matters during 1919 that must have concerned most Bramcote residents as they threatened changes to the status quo. It seems likely that the majority of people united in a strong protest, led by the Parish Council, against a plan to incorporate Bramcote in the City of Nottingham. They decided on taking "all steps possible to resist this annexation" and invited the neighbouring villages to join in their protest. By the end of the year a letter had been sent to the Ministry of Health and also to Stapleford Rural District Council stating that the Parish Council saw no justification for the inclusion of a small, purely agricultural parish of 1,064 acres, with a scattered population of between six and seven hundred, to be absorbed into the city's area. Some ninety plus years later, and despite further attempts to make us city dwellers, we have managed to maintain our ancestors' line of defence and Bramcote is still located in Nottinghamshire rather than Nottingham.

Ivy House, Church Street

The second change could not be resisted, however, as Major Ernest Frank Holden of Bramcote Hills offered much of his Bramcote and Stapleford estate for sale on Wednesday 28th May. The Major was not living in the village, having relocated to Scalby Hall near Scarborough and presumably he wished to reduce his commitments in the area.

The properties auctioned at The Welbeck Hotel in Nottingham included Common Lane Farm, The Old Manor House Farm, The Sherwin Arms, The Grange, Ivy House, The Post Office shop/cottage, The Smithy and many other cottages, gardens and other parcels of land. This gave the opportunity for several Bramcote residents to become house owners instead of tenants e.g. Ellis Hallam Joule, the tenant at The Manor House purchased it for £6,000, Henry Taylor bought Common Lane Farm for £3,500 and Nathan Woodward became the owner of The Sherwin Arms at a cost of £4,600. Many of those in smaller properties, however, must have felt very vulnerable and would have worried as to who their new landlord would be and how their rents would be affected.

The Post Office and shop, Town Street

Thus at the end of this year the village itself would have appeared little changed but there were subtle differences to people's life styles and expectations with, perhaps overall, a greater sense of hope.

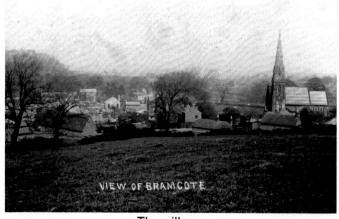

The village

1920 – Remembrance

Even as servicemen settled back into regular employment or sought new work opportunities, reminders of what they had experienced were constant. Many men had not been discharged until 1919 with some, like John Jesse Burton, being sent home permanently disabled and others returning with mental and physical traumas.

Lt. Col. Noel Pearson D.S.O.,M.C.

More uplifting for the community as a whole, must have been the receipt of medals and honours such as the Distinguished Service Order and Military Cross awarded to Lt. Col. Noel Pearson. The O.B.E. medal given to a Bramcote woman, Florence Jackson, in February 1920, received limited publicity but suggests that the village nurtured a very brave young woman. In the 1911 census there is nothing to suggest that Florrie was in any way exceptional. She was recorded as being 19 and working as a bookkeeper, living in a house on Derby Road with her parents and four younger siblings. During the war, however, she joined Queen Mary's Army Auxiliary Corps and saw service abroad, receiving her honour for the work she undertook on the French front. Florrie went on to marry Gordon King Chitty at St. Michael's Church in 1923 and they moved to the London area. Unfortunately we have not been able to locate any of her family or any photographs though we believe that she died in Epping in 1972.

Sadly February brought a much more poignant reminder of the war with the death, as a result of his injuries, of William Harris and many attended his military funeral at the church.

The desire to have a memorial, within the church, to those who had lost their lives meant that fund raising efforts continued. One such venture was a performance of a play written by local man Stanley Briggs. Called "The Profiteer" and featuring characters such as Mr. Graball, Tom Sharp and Annie Flat, it was performed in the schoolroom on a Saturday evening to such acclaim that £8 was raised and a repeat performance demanded on the next Saturday.

Stanley and Kathleen Briggs
with their daughter, Patricia

Another social event at which donations might have been sought was organised by the evening school that had been started in the autumn of the previous year, under the direction of Mr. Twells of Trowell. Combined with a prize-giving there was a varied bill of entertainment including an elocutionist, pianists and singers plus dancing and games in which all could participate.

It was in mid April that the war memorial in St. Michael's Church was finally unveiled in what The Stapleford and Sandiacre Reporter entitled "An Impressive Ceremony". The journalist clearly found the occasion momentous so it seems appropriate to quote from his article:

> "Never within living remembrance has the pretty little church at Bramcote been so crowded as it was on Sunday afternoon last, the occasion being the unveiling of a memorial tablet to the memory of those gallant sons of Bramcote who laid down their lives in The Great War. That 15 out of this small and peaceful village should have laid down their lives in defence of the flag of freedom is an honour that cannot be adequately expressed in words."

The service was conducted by The Reverend W.M. Browne, the vicar, whose prayer after the solemn unveiling included the words: *"Accept this offering at our hands in remembrance of our brethren who gave their lives in the war"*. The Reverend J.P. Hales, Rector of Cotgrave, preached a "manly and touching sermon". Both "The Last Post" and "The Reveille" were played in what was called "a truly impressive service".

Ironically it was some days after this event that the vicar plus Noel Gervis Pearson and George Jackson, the churchwardens, sought a faculty (i.e. permission from the church authorities) *"to provide and place on a large pillar a bronze war memorial tablet to the glory of God and in grateful memory of the men of Bramcote who gave their lives for England and honour in the Great War 1914-18 --- with their names --- and the inscription: "the souls of the righteous are in the hand of God" "*.

In June 1920 it was announced in the church magazine that the secretary for the Imperial War Graves Commission would receive applications from the next of kin of soldiers buried in France for the original wooden crosses when they were replaced by more permanent memorials. The vicar made it clear that arrangements could be made to have them placed in the churchyard. It is only in very recent years that the remaining wooden cross disappeared.

It is hoped that, although artefacts will wither and disappear over the decades, the stories of how Bramcote families were affected by a world war, whether abroad or at home, will continue to be explored and recorded with appreciation of their resilience.

St. Michael's Church

The Glorious Dead

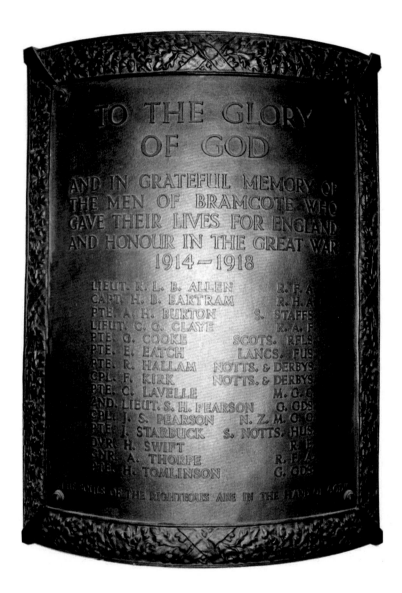

The memorial plaque in St. Michael's Church, Bramcote

Richard Lancelot Baugh Allen 1887- 27.12.1918
Lieutenant, Royal Field Artillery

Richard was the only child of Wilfred and Annie Baugh Allen and was born in Chelsea, London. Wilfred, a barrister, had married Annie Sophia Wedgwood, great grand-daughter of Josiah Wedgwood, on 26th December 1883 at Stanton in Gloucestershire. Richard attended Eton School.

Wilfred was appointed a judge on 22nd January 1903. The first time he is on the electoral roll for Bramcote is 1906 when he was living at Southfield House. On the 1911 census he is recorded as having 5 servants. In Wright's Directory for 1915-6 Wilfred Baugh Allen is listed as a judge at the County Court, St. Peter's Gate, Nottingham, with his home in Bramcote. In 1917 he resigned and moved to "Rosemount," Tenby.

Southfield House

On the 1911 census Richard was living at 18 Emperor's Gate, Kensington as a boarder in an apartment house. He was a 23 year old single man. On 11th April 1915 Richard returned to Liverpool from New York on the Lusitania. According to the Cunard log he was a barrister aged 28 years and had been living in Canada.

In the June quarter of 1917 Richard married Marion Irvine at Preston, Lancashire. It is to be his wife who applies for her late husband's medals on 6th January 1921.

As well as being on the Bramcote memorial in St. Michael's Church, Richard is remembered on the Lampeter Velfry War Memorial, Pembroke, and the following information is taken from their website:

> "Richard Lancelot Baugh Allen, Lieutenant, Royal Field Artillery. Richard had received a commission into the Royal Field Artillery, and was posted to the 67th Brigade, RFA, Éwhich was attached to the 13th (Western) Division. The Division moved to Mudros in July, 1915 and from there moved to Gallipoli between the 6th to the 16th July, landing at Cape Helles. The Division then moved to the ANZAC sector, and fought at the Battles of Sari Bair, Russell's Top, and Hill 60. They moved again, to Suvla, and on the 15th October 1915 the 67th Brigade, RFA joined the 10th Division in Salonika. They remained in Salonika until early September, 1917 when they moved to Egypt. They then spent the remainder of the war fighting in Palestine. At the end of the war they moved back to Cairo. Richard died of illness here on the 27th December, 1918 aged 31, and is buried at Cairo War Memorial Cemetery, Egypt." Grave/Reference Number M217.

At the Cairo War Memorial Cemetery 2,057 Commonwealth casualties of the First World War are buried or commemorated. At the outbreak of the war Cairo was headquarters to the United Kingdom garrison in Egypt. With Alexandria, it became the main hospital centre for Gallipoli in 1915 and later dealt with the sick and wounded from operations in Egypt and Palestine.

Cairo War Memorial Cemetery courtesy of
Commonwealth War Graves Commission (www.cwgc.org)

Harry Brocklesby Bartram 17.9.1877 – 16.9.1914
Captain, Royal Horse Artillery

Harry was born in Tunbridge Wells on 17th September 1877, the only son of the Reverend Henry Bartram, Vicar of St. Mary the Virgin, Dover, Rural Dean of Dover and Canon of Canterbury, and his wife Amy.

Harry embarked on a military career. He had attained the rank of Lieutenant in the Royal Horse Artillery by the time of his marriage to Alice Eugenia Smith of Bramcote Hall in July 1907 at Trinity Church, Chelsea. Alice was the daughter of Frederic Chatfield Smith known locally as "Banker Smith". Harry and Alice had three children, Diana, Elizabeth and Harry Bob, born only days after the death of his father. Harry Bob was also to lose his life whilst fighting for his country in 1941.

Captain Bartram

After returning from India in December 1913, Harry Bartram, Captain of E Battery, Royal Horse Artillery, 3rd Cavalry Brigade was stationed in Ireland. A member of Britain's small, highly professional, regular army, he and his battery were amongst the first to arrive in France after the declaration of war.

Captain Bartram and E Battery sailed on the S.S. Pancras, leaving to much fanfare and flag waving, and landed in France on 17th August 1914. After disembarking at Havre, his batttery, men and horses had to make the journey from France to Belgium, where fighting was to take place, arriving four days later on 21st August at 9pm which was "too late for tea".

It was the guns of E Battery that were to be the first fired in the campaign, at 11.10am on Saturday 22nd August 1914, near Bray in Belgium.

During the first days of the war, Captain Bartram and his battery, although outnumbered, fought daily at the Battle of Mons. Such continuous and prolonged fighting left little or no time for normal activities like food and rest.

His father was later quoted as saying that Captain Bartram's Battery went 36 hours without food, there being no time for a proper meal because of continuous fighting day and night.

Captain Bartram, known as "Barter", was meticulous in keeping a diary of his war service which was published for private circulation in 1915. The published work is called "Diary of the Retirement from Mons August 1914" by Capt. Harry Brocklesby Bartram ('Barter').

It is through this diary that we are able to know some fascinating details of his life in France and Belgium in the early days of World War One.

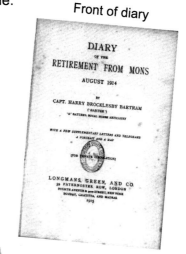

Front of diary

Diary extracts –

(Diary entry made after arrival in France)
"Aug 18th ....was presented by a little man with a strip of tricolour ribbon, which I stuck in my cap...later...a young lady gave me a chrysanthemum which I wore in my coat ..!"

Once fighting began, the tone of his diary changes

(letter to his wife from the front in Belgium)
"Aug 23rd ....we are all just about done in and are badly in need of rest.....We were in action yesterday...Up at 2.30am yesterday, to bed at 4am this morning, fighting all day and a twenty-mile march after dark.."

(Diary extracts from the front in Belgium)
"Aug 26th ....I went absolutely fast asleep on Old Paddy...every man practically asleep in the saddle..."
"Aug 28th ....no rations ..."
"Aug 29th ...rations arrived but ordered to move before had any food..."
The diary has an abrupt end ....

Back of diary

Captain Bartram collapsed with gastritis on 30th August 1914 following his "privations in the field" and was invalided back to England to recover. Unfortunately, it took nine days travel in various motor vehicles to reach the Alexandra Hospital, Cosham. It was then too late and he succumbed to his illness, dying on 16th September 1914, just short of his 36th birthday. He was buried in Dover (St. Mary's) New Cemetery, Kent on 19th September, grave ref: E.H.12.

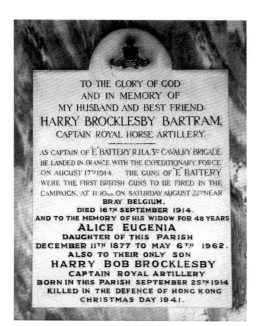

Telegram to Captain Bartram's wife (extract) Sept.18th
"Deeply regret to inform you that Captain H.B.Bartram, R.H.A., died at the Alexandra Hospital, Cosham,...on the morning of 16th Sept. Lord Kitchener expresses his sympathy."
SECRETARY, WAR OFFICE.

This memorial to Captain Bartram is in St. Michael and All Angels Church, Bramcote.

Arthur Henry Burton 1898 - 24.3.1918

Private, 2nd Battalion, South Staffordshire Regiment
Service Number 202194

Arthur was born in Bramcote, the son of Peter and Mary Burton. He had 5 brothers, one of whom died as a baby, 3 stepbrothers, 1 sister and 1 stepsister, his father Peter having been widowed and then remarried.

Peter was a joiner and the family lived in Broomhill Terrace, Derby Road, followed by Town Street, and by the 1911 census they had moved to "The Cottage" known today as "The Gables" on Main Street and Peter was working for Major Holden as an estate joiner. Peter served on Bramcote Parish Council from 1896 to 1903 and again from 1915 to 1919.

Wedding of Florence Burton and James Cook 1903 Bramcote
Arthur is sitting front row far left

Arthur enlisted at Ilkeston, and joined the South Staffordshire Regiment. He served with the 2nd Battalion and was "killed in action" near Arras in France aged 20 years. This was at the time of the German offensive codenamed "Operation Michael" when the entire British sector of the Western Front was bombarded by shells and then attacked by German storm troopers.

He is remembered on The Arras Memorial which commemorates almost 35,000 servicemen from the United Kingdom, South Africa and New Zealand who were killed in the Arras sector and have no known grave.

There is a private memorial stone to him in Bramcote churchyard, erected by his parents, where it states that "He was one of six soldier sons that answered their country's call." We have traced records for two of these brothers, John Jesse Burton and Cyril Burton, but have no evidence for any of the others.

Arthur Henry Burton's grave in Bramcote churchyard
and below the wording on the cross

"WHEN FREEDOM BELLS FOR VICTORY RING
AND PEACE IS OURS AGAIN,
WE'LL SAY WITHIN OUR HEARTS THAT DAY
HE DID NOT DIE IN VAIN."

Charles Geoffrey Claye 14.2.1895 - 5.7.1918
Flying Officer, 99 Squadron Royal Flying Corps

Charles was born at "The Hall," Radcliffe-on-Trent, the only son of Ernest Wentworth Claye and his wife Mary and he had a younger sister Dorothy. On the 1901 census Ernest was a railway rolling stock manufacturer. The family moved to Bramcote Hills House in 1908, Lenton House, Nottingham in 1916 and in 1919 to "The Hill," East Bridgford, Nottinghamshire.

Bramcote Hills House

"The Hill", East Bridgford

Charles was educated at Hinwick House School, Wellingborough, and at Charterhouse School. On the 1911 census Charles, aged 16, was a patient in the sanatorium at Charterhouse School, and his father was a manager and director of the Railway Wagon Works, Long Eaton.

In September 1914 Charles received his commission in the 5th Battalion Sherwood Foresters, and went to the front in August 1916. He transferred to the Royal Flying Corps on 6th March 1917 and was accepted to train as an observer. Following training he was attached to No. 48 Squadron and during this period in 1917 he was wounded twice. Reconnaissance missions were dangerous and usually carried out by a crew of two. The pilot was required to fly straight and level to allow the observer to take a series of overlapping photographs recording the location of enemy troop movements, artillery positions, trench lines, wire defences and any other useful information, reporting this back upon landing. The planes on these missions were an easy target for anti-aircraft guns and stalking fighters.

The D.H.9 aircraft in which Charles flew

After being seconded for temporary duties with other squadrons, Charles was appointed to Flying Officer Observer with seniority, effective from 13th April 1917. Some home leave was taken during the period 17th November to the 1st December 1917 following which Flying Officer Claye was given a 'home' posting. He re-embarked for the front on 20th April 1918 on being appointed to serve with No. 99 Squadron. This squadron was engaged on long distance bombing raids into Germany in the course of which it suffered very heavy casualties. The aircraft in which Charles flew as an observer was a D.H.9

Flying Officer Claye was aged 23 when he was killed in action on 5th July 1918, acting as an observer in a raid over Kaiserslanten. He is buried at Charmes Military Cemetery, Essegney Vosges, France. Grave/Reference Number 1A.B.

Charles is also remembered in the Memorial Chapel at Charterhouse School, and the Lenton War Memorial, Nottingham. He was further commemorated by means of an endowed bed at the old Nottingham General Hospital on The Ropewalk.

George Cooke 1890 - 13.7.1916

Private, 9th Battalion Cameronians (Scottish Rifles)

Service Number 16778

Joseph George Cooke was born at Epperstone, Notts, the youngest son of Thomas and Sarah Cooke and baptised there 1st June 1890. He had 4 brothers: Ernest, James, Albert and Harold and a sister, Kate Mabel. By the 1901 census the family were living at The Courtyard, off Cow Lane, Bramcote, and Thomas was a farm bailiff   .

The 1911 census sees the family of Thomas and Sarah with their sons Ernest, James, and George and a granddaughter Millicent living on Main Street at Bramcote. Thomas and Sarah had been married 46 years. Although 78 years old, Thomas was still a nurseryman and George aged 21 years, had followed him into that trade.

George enlisted at Ilkeston in the Cameronians (Scottish Rifles) on 11th January 1915. He went to France with the 9th Battalion landing at Boulogne on 12th May 1915. The 9th Scottish Division served on the Western Front throughout the war and was regarded by many as one of the best fighting formations in the 1914-18 conflicts.

George survived the first major engagement involving the 9th Division, the Battle of Loos. On the opening day alone, 25th September 1915, over 150 men of the 9th Scottish Rifles were killed. The next action in which the 9th Division took part was the Battle of the Somme in July 1916; the Scottish Rifles had 40 men killed in the first week. The battalion was in ready to take part on the opening day of the Battle of Bazentin, when George, aged 26, was killed in action by artillery fire on 13th July.

George Cooke

The Beeston Gazette of 2nd September 1916 printed this article:

Death of Bramcote Hero

We regret to record the death of Private George Cooke of the Scottish Rifles, aged 25, the youngest son of Mr. and Mrs Thomas Cooke of Bramcote. Previous to the war he was employed at the Stanton Iron Works, but joined the Scottish Rifles in January 1915. After four months training he was sent out to France, and took part in several battles. He was granted a short leave in May last, but returned to take part in the big push. It was while holding one of the villages taken from the Germans, and guarding it against counter attack that Cooke met his death through the bursting of a shrapnel shell on 13th July.

A letter of sympathy has been received from the lieutenant of his regiment assuring his mother and family that he was much missed by his comrades and that he was one of the best soldiers. His loss is deeply felt by his sorrowing family and fiancée Miss Eva Paling.

In the same edition in the announcements column was the following:

Oh we miss him, oh how sadly,
Sorrowing hearts alone can tell
Earth has lost him, heaven has gained him
Jesus has done all things well.
From his sorrowing family and fiancée Eva.

(Eva married Harold, George's brother, on the 14th September 1918 at Beeston.)

George is remembered on the Thiepval Memorial. Grave/reference number pier and face 4D. This memorial is the largest memorial built by the Commonwealth War Graves Commission and commemorates more than 72,000 officers and men of the United Kingdom and South African forces who died in the Somme sector before 20th March 1918, and have no known grave. Over 90% of those commemorated died between July and November 1916.

Thiepval Memorial
courtesy of Commonwealth War Graves Commission (www.cwgc.org)

Three of his brothers, Ernest (Motor Transport Company of the Army Service Corps) James (4th Battalion Sherwood Foresters) and Harold (Royal Field Artillery) all returned home safely.

Ernest Eatch 23.9.1888 – 23.10.1916

Private, 2nd Battalion Lancashire Fusiliers

Service number 37074

Ernest, born in Bramcote, probably at Ivy House on Church Street, was the son of Francis and Flora Eatch. The family had long been shopkeepers and bakers in the village but by 1911, they had also become the village butchers. The butcher's shop was below the entrance to King George V's Park on Main Street, now called Town Street.

Butcher's shop on Main Street

A member of the Bramcote Village Health and Strength Club before The Great War, Ernest enlisted at Derby, joining the North Staffordshire Regiment. He later transferred to the Lancashire Fusiliers and served with the 2nd Battalion in France, taking part in the Battle of the Somme in 1916.

Delville Wood, which lay on a ridge of high ground to the north east of the River Somme, was a crucial British target. One of many woods in the area, it had been the site of frequent assaults and enormous losses since the start of battle in July 1916.

Ernest Eatch 1909

Ernest was killed at Delville Wood on 23rd October 1916, aged 28. Like so many who perished fighting on the Somme, he has no known grave but is remembered with honour on the Thiepval Memorial (ref: Pier and Face 3 C and 3 D)

Certificate in memory of Private Eatch

Pictured below are the medals
awarded to Ernest Eatch

War Medal   Victory Medal

His Memorial Medal
and Certificate
(issued after the war
to the bereaved family)

Richard Hallam 1879 – 22.3.1918
Corporal, 15th Battalion Sherwood Foresters
Service Number 24116

Richard was born to George and Elizabeth Hallam from Stapleford. He had 16 brothers and sisters and was in fact the second son of George and Elizabeth to be christened with the name of Richard. They had previously had a son who was born in 1863 and who had died in April 1879 at the age of 16 of typhoid fever, only a few months before the second Richard was born.

In June 1914 he married Hannah Edwards who lived with her parents on Chapel Street, Bramcote. The 1871 census shows Hannah's grandparents as being the publicans of "The White Lion" on Town Street. Richard and Hannah had a son, George William.

Richard could not join the army at the outbreak of World War One as he was below the standard military height so he continued to work as a labourer at Stanton Ironworks. However, with the ever increasing demand for more and more men to join Kitchener's Army, the Bantam battalions were formed. These units were made up of men who although fit, were below the normal minimum service height of 5'3". Richard enlisted in the 15th Battalion Sherwood Foresters in early March 1915. The Battalion landed in France on 1st February 1916.

Hannah and George

On 21st March 1918 the enemy launched its largest offensive of the war on the Somme, known as the "Kaiserschlacht". This offensive was designed to destroy the overstretched British Fifth Army and to split the British and French armies. Richard was killed in action on 22nd March 1918 during a German attack on the trenches at Curlu Wood, France, whilst serving with HQ Company of the 15th Battalion. He is buried in the Roisel Communal Cemetery Extension, Somme, France Grave/Reference Number 111.D.16.

Richard Hallam

After the death of Richard in 1918, Hannah, along with her family and friends in Bramcote, decided to change the name of their son from George Hallam to Dick Hallam in memory of her late husband and he was known by this name until his death in 1989.

Frank Kirk 1892 – 21.3.1918

Corporal, 2/5th Battalion Sherwood Foresters
Service Number 20284

Frank Kirk was the second son of William and Minnie Kirk. Their first son, also named Frank, died aged one day in March 1890, and, as was common practice they used the name again when their second son was born. He also had an older sister Kathleen. By the 1901 census they were all living on Common Lane, Bramcote, and William was a yard man on a farm.

The 1911 census shows the family living at Rose Cottage. William was now a coal carter, Kathleen a dressmaker and Frank a grocer's assistant.

Frank enlisted on 1st December 1915 at Derby in the 2nd/5th Battalion Sherwood Foresters, Nottinghamshire and Derbyshire Regiment. He was 23 years old and still a grocer's assistant working for Ilkeston Co-op in Park Road, Ilkeston, but now living at 54 Northwood Street, Stapleford, with his family. He was mobilised on 9th February 1916, and served with HQ Company. He went to France in February 1917 and was soon promoted to Lance Corporal, and then Corporal.

Embroidered silk cards were hand-stitched by French and Belgian women and were sent by soldiers to their families back home.

He was reported missing in action on 1st March 1918, following the German attack on the lines at Noreuil/Ervillers France. Corporal Kirk is recorded as having died on 21st March 1918 aged 25 and is buried at Arras Memorial Park, Pas de Calais, France.

His service calculated to this date was given as two years, one hundred and eleven days. At the time of his death his parents were living at Sandboro Fields, Risley.

Frank was the first of three men from Bramcote to die within four days during this battle, the others being Arthur Burton and Richard Hallam.

Charles Patton Lavelle 12.1.1893 – 1.7.1916

Private, 103rd Company Machine Gun Corps (Infantry)
Service Number 13011

Charles Lavelle was born in Lythe, near Whitby, Yorkshire where his father worked as gamekeeper for the Marquis of Normanby. Charles was the only son of Patrick and Eliza, an Irish couple, who also had four daughters. In 1904, they moved to Bramcote when Patrick became gamekeeper to the Holden family at Bramcote Hills. Charlie, as he was known, followed his father's occupation and by 1911 was also a gamekeeper.

Family Group (l-r) Charles, Patrick, Lily,Greta, Eliza, Nora, Kathleen

Charles in uniform

Charlie enlisted with the Sherwood Foresters in March 1915 and was posted for service overseas in August of that year. He sailed from Devonport to the Dardanelles on R.M.S. Empress of Britain.

He served with the 9th Battalion at Gallipoli where sea and land battles were fought to protect the only naval route from the Mediterranean to the Black Sea. The campaign was a failure, ending in withdrawal during January 1916. Charlie was listed as wounded in The Times casualty list published 19th October 1915. The standard delay in the publication of these lists suggests that Charlie was wounded about mid September. At this time the 9th Battalion were in rest camp but were providing working parties in the front line trenches, suffering considerable casualties in the process. Charlie was evacuated to England and on his recovery joined the 3rd Battalion on 31st January 1916.

Some postcards and letters Charlie sent or received during his war experience have survived.

In one letter sent just before his last posting and dated 3rd February 1916, Charlie is newly based in Sunderland along with many of his pals who had returned from the fighting in the Dardenelles. He mentions the Zeppelins which were "rather close" to Bramcote the previous Monday and says the billet in Sunderland is "not very comfortable" and is kept "awful dark at night…just like walking in a wood".

Postcard sent by Charlie 24th August 1915
"Tuesday
Dear Mother
This is a pic of the ship that has to take us to the Dardanelles. We came aboard at Devonport this morning. We are close to Camels Head.
Best love to all from your loving
Charlie"

Extract of card sent by sister Greta
"Dear Charlie
Hope you are all right.
…. Hope you will get parcel safe you will think you have got hlf a stone of flour. Stanley has printed the address on one side & Ma on the other side + she has sewn it up well so you'll have to get your bayonet to work to get it open…..sorry we could not get everything in the parcel there was some cocoa + tinned milk choc wafers but we send them another time…….
With best wishes from your loving sister Greta"

Charlie was posted to the Machine Gun Corps on 21st February 1916. He served in France with the 103rd Company as part of the 34th Division. He was killed in action on the 1st July 1916, the opening day of the infamous Battle of the Somme, along with eighteen comrades in the 103rd Company. Charles is buried in the Gordon Dump Cemetery, Ovillers-La-Biossell. He is commemorated on a special memorial, reference Sp.Mem.B.19.

Memorials to Charlie.

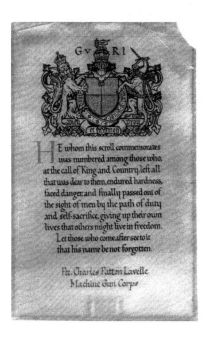

Stephen Hetley Pearson 30.6.1882 – 1.12.1917
2nd Lieutenant, 2nd Battalion Grenadier Guards

Stephen Hetley and his brother John Strachan were the twin sons of Henry John Pearson and his wife Laura. The brothers were born in Beeston, later moving to The White House in Bramcote with their family. The family consisted of three brothers, all of whom served time in the military, and four sisters. Stephen, known as "Hetley", was educated at Charterhouse School and trained as an articled chartered accountant, later becoming a director of the family-run Beeston Foundry Company.

Hetley Pearson 1906

Beeston Lads' Club

Keenly interested in the welfare of local youngsters, in 1909, he was instrumental in the re-forming of the 17th Nottingham (Beeston) Boys' Brigade of which he was Captain and a "Big Brother" to all the lads who gave him the affectionate name of "Mr Hetley". Following the death of his father in 1913, Hetley made a generous donation to establish the Lads' Club on Station Road in Beeston as a permanent home for his brigade.

After the outbreak of war Hetley had deeds drawn up providing an endowment of £10,000 and establishing trustees to ensure the Boys' Brigade in Beeston would continue in his absence. The content of his letters sent back to the brigade show how, even in the midst of war, his thoughts remained with them all.

Hetley Pearson
Captain of the Boys' Brigade

Hetley was living at The Limes in Chilwell when he attested on 9th December 1915. He was mobilised in April 1916 and posted to the 28th (Reserve) Battalion Northumberland Fusiliers. Initially he served at Cramlington with the 28th Battalion and was promoted rapidly during 1916, eventually being recommended for a commission. He was gazetted 2nd Lieutenant with the Grenadier Guards on 15th January 1917. He went to the frontline in France but maintained contact by letter with the Boys' Brigade whenever he could do so.

Lieutenant Hetley Pearson

On 1st December 1917, during the battle for Gauche Wood, 2nd Lieutenant Stephen Hetley Pearson was shot in the head whilst leading his men and died immediately. The battle resulted in many deaths and other casualties and in the ensuing confusion his body was not identified. Tributes by his fellow officers following his death described him as "a gallant gentleman" and "a fine leader of great bravery".

A well attended memorial service was held at the Beeston Parish Church at which the Boys' Brigade bugle band played "The Last Post" and a muffled peal was rung on the bells.

Despite many lengthy efforts by his family to find his grave no trace could be found. However, seven years after his death, several isolated graves in the region of Gauche Wood were moved to permanent cemeteries and his remains were finally identified from a handkerchief found upon his body which bore the initials "S.H.P.".

Stephen Hetley Pearson was finally buried in Villers Faucon, Communal Cemetery Extension in Grave 6, Row A, Plot 4.

Other permanent memorials to 2nd Lieutenant S.H. Pearson:-

Plaques
Charterhouse School
Beeston Boys' Brigade

Bells
St. Mary's Church, Attenborough

Stained Glass Window
St. Michael & All Angels Church, Bramcote

John Strachan Pearson 30.6.1882 – 4.11.1918

Corporal, New Zealand Mounted Machine Gun Corps
Service Number 13/2236

John Strachan was one of twin boys born to Laura Kate and Henry John Pearson in Beeston. The family consisting of John, his twin brother Stephen Hetley, younger brother Noel Gervis and four sisters later moved to Bramcote to take up residence at "The White House", Town Street (now known as Bramcote Nursing Home). Their father Henry was a successful businessman, having established the Beeston Foundry Company in 1888 but by 1901 John was working as a farmer.

John, also known as Jack, emigrated, probably in November 1910, with the intention of becoming a fruit farmer in Australia. Little is known of his life in Australia but he did travel on to New Zealand where he settled in a remote mission station called Mangawhare near Tangiteroia, Auckland and is said to have been a sheep farmer.

John enlisted into the Auckland Mounted Rifles in 1915 and embarked for Suez, Egypt on 14th August 1915 as a trooper. He served in the region during the ill-fated Gallipoli campaign and in Palestine where he contracted malaria. Three years later, after much fighting against the Turks, John, now Corporal Pearson, was serving with the Mounted Machine Gun Corps in Egypt when he was taken ill again. His condition deteriorated rapidly and on 2nd November he was admitted to the 17th General Hospital in Alexandria where he died of malaria two days later.

Corporal Pearson is buried in the Alexandria (Hadra) War Memorial Cemetery, Egypt, grave reference A. 177.

Having remained single, John left his entire estate to his mother in England. For the next forty years, an "In Memoriam" notice was placed in "The Times" every year on the anniversary of the deaths of the twin sons, John Strachan and Stephen Hetley Pearson which ended with the words: "Their name liveth for ever more".

Other permanent memorials to
Corporal J.S. Pearson:-

Plaques
Upper Wairoa District War Memorial,
Tangiteroria, North Island, New Zealand.

Bells
St. Mary's Church, Attenborough.

Stained Glass Window
St. Michael and All Angels Church, Bramcote.

Stained Glass Window

John Starbuck 1881 – 23.12.1917

Private, South Nottinghamshire Hussars
Service Number 280232

John was born at Bramcote in 1881 to John and Martha Starbuck. On the 1881 census the family were living on Church Street, John was a coal miner and John junior was one month old. He had two older siblings, Charles and Mary. The 1891 census saw the family living on Main Street and there were four more children: William, Edna, James and Walter. By 1901 the family had moved to Cow Lane and John, aged 20 years, was a horse driver in a coal mine.

John married Clara Francis and on the 1911 census they were living with their son Cyril, aged 1 year, as boarders at 11 Chapel Street, Stapleford. John was now a collier hewer.

John joined the South Nottinghamshire Hussars at the outbreak of the war, enlisting at Stapleford, and according to the regimental records, embarked at Avonmouth on 8th April 1915, arriving at Alexandria on 24th April 1915.

During his service Private Starbuck is believed to have fought against the Turks at Gallipoli, against the Bulgarians in Northern Greece and then against the Turks again in what is now known as the Gaza Strip, the objective being to capture Jerusalem. During this latter engagement on 29th/30th November 1917 there was heavy fighting during which the South Notts. suffered a number of casualties, some of the wounded being transferred to hospital in Egypt.

Private Starbuck died in Egypt on 23rd December 1917. He is buried at Kantara War Cemetery. Grave/Reference Number Row C Grave 137.

Kantara War Cemetery
courtesy of Commonwealth War Graves Commission (www.cwgc.org)

There is some confusion about John's records. There are two medal cards, one for John Starbuck where his wife applied for his 1914 Star, and one for John Starbrook who was awarded the British, Victory and 15 Star medals. His Commonwealth War Grave Certificate shows the name Starbrook. Both have the same service number.

Harry Swift 1876 – 11.5.1918

Driver, Royal Engineers

Service Number 52705

Harry was born in Bramcote to Andrew and Sarah Swift. He had three brothers: William, Walter and George and a sister Amy. The family lived at 32 Town Street. He started work as a gardener, but on the 1901 census Harry was at Glossop Hall, Derbyshire, working as a stable helper.

Bramcote Parish Council minute book shows that Harry was co-opted onto the Council on 9th January 1908 to fill a vacancy left by William Moore. He was then elected to the council for three years in April 1910.

Harry married Mary Ann Clake on 6th June 1908 at the Parish Church of St. Mark in Barrow in Furness. Harry, aged 30 years, was a carpenter and his bride was 27 years old. Andrew Swift, his father, was described as a gentleman, and Mary's father Thorold was an engine driver.

On the 1911 census Harry and Mary were living on Main Street, Bramcote with their children: Winifred aged 2 years and George aged 2 months. Harry was a carpenter's labourer. Harry and Mary had two more sons: Walter born in 1913 and Henry born in 1918 and who was never to see his father.

Harry Swift's wife Mary
and three of their children

On 9th September 1914 Harry applied to join the army at the Nottingham Recruiting Office. At the time he was described as a horse driver. However the Commanding Officer felt that although he was a "strong active man," Harry was too old to join up, and his application was declined. He was aged 36 years. A few days later the officer did send a memo to the Chatham Record Office asking that Harry be retained as a driver for the Royal Engineers as he was "used to horses and had been engaged as a civilian groom to army officers." He was accepted as a driver, and Harry joined the Royal Engineers on 21st September.

Harry in uniform

Harry served at home until July 1915 and then embarked for France. He was a member of the 19th Division Signal Company. The Royal Engineers maintained the telephones, wireless and other signalling equipment, and provided technical expertise at the frontline.

He was invalided to a hospital in Devonport on 4th May 1918, and died there on the 11th May. He was buried in St. Michael's Churchyard to the west of the church on 16th May.

After Harry's death Mary was awarded a pension of 33/9d a week for her and their four children. Life must have been very hard for all of them.

Harry's memorial in the churchyard

Harry's mother at the almshouses

Albert Thorpe 1896 – 19.3.1915

Driver, 1st Reserve Battery, Royal Field Artillery

Service Number 34597

The first we know of Albert in Bramcote is on the 1911 census when he was 14 years old and living in Chapel Street with his parents, Albert and Sarah, and younger sister, Mary. He enlisted at Ilkeston in January 1915 and was then sent to Newcastle.

At the Nottinghamshire Archives there is a folder of letters and other information related to Albert. The letters are addressed to Mrs Thorpe, Church Street, Bramcote. They are all signed "from your loving son Albert" with lots of kisses.

His first letter home is dated 14th January 1915.

"I hope you are all well because I am as happy as a king. We have sausage and taties for breakfast with tea, meat and potatoes and soup for dinner, cake, bread and butter for tea, and nothing to do. We shall have our kit tomorrow and I will send my boots and coat home."

29th January 1915

"The parson sent me a little bible with a letter which I will send to you. He was sorry to hear that Mary is ill. I hope you have got rid of your colds and are well and strong. You want to be up here it is a lot colder than where you are. We are only 10 miles from the sea; aeroplanes fly over the barracks every day. I have been building sheds and been close to one when it rose. There is a free supper every Sunday and Wednesday nights at Brunswick Chapel which I go to."He is very proud when on Church parade with the band playing on Sunday. "It is a fine sight."

He writes home regularly asking his mum to send him cigarettes, chocolate, a comic paper and a picture of "our Mary". Once he had his uniform he felt much happier, saying he had plenty to eat, and that he would be able to send money home.

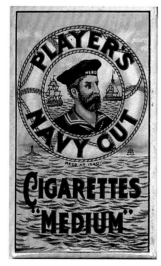

Courtesy of Nottingham City Museums and Galleries.

Sadly Albert was not to see any action because he died on 19th March from meningitis in the Newcastle City Hospital for Infectious Diseases.

The Ilkeston Pioneer newspaper printed the following article on 26th March:

Nottingham Soldier's death at Newcastle

"On Monday 22nd March the funeral of the late Gunner Albert Thorpe, RFA, took place from the hospital at Walker Gate, Newcastle-on-Tyne. The deceased was buried with full military honours, the procession being followed by a large number of men from his regiment. The Dead March in Saul was played by the band on the way to St. Andrew's Cemetery, and after the funeral rites had been performed three volleys were fired over the grave, after which the buglers sounded The Last Post. Gunner Thorpe a native of Bramcote, Nottingham, was a young man of great promise and greatly respected by his comrades in the RFA at Newcastle."

St. Andrew's Cemetery contains 183 First World War burials, about half of them in a war graves' plot.

St. Andrew's Cemetery, Newcastle-Upon-Tyne. Photograph courtesy of
The Commonwealth War Graves Commission. (www.cwgc.org)

Harry Tomlinson 1885 – 26.9.1916

Private, 4th Battalion Grenadier Guards

Service Number 22051

Harry was the son of William and Ada Tomlinson and had three sisters Martha, Edith and Julia and two brothers William and Jesse. On the 1901 census he was 15 and a colliery labourer, having followed his father and brothers into the mines.

On 3rd February 1908 he married Gertrude Smith and his marriage certificate shows that at this time he was a police constable, but two years later he returned to the pits as a miner. By the 1911 census Harry and his family were living on Chapel Street, Bramcote. Harry and Gertrude had two children, Herbert aged 2 years and Kate aged 11 months.

Harry and his brother enlisted together with the Grenadier Guards in January 1915. Both men went to France in October of that year and saw action on the Somme battlefields. Harry died of his wounds in France on 26th September 1916. He is buried at Grove Town Cemetery, Meaulte. Ref: IG16.

There is a brass plaque in the entrance porch of St. Michael's Church that reads "From his grave in France, In Loving memory of Harry Tomlinson, Love Never Faileth"

Their brother William served as a special constable in Bramcote. Jesse survived the war; he had been a miner like Harry, but later he became the licensee of The White Lion.

Harry's grave,
Grove Town Cemetery, Meaulte.

Jesse, grandfather William and William

Names on a Memorial

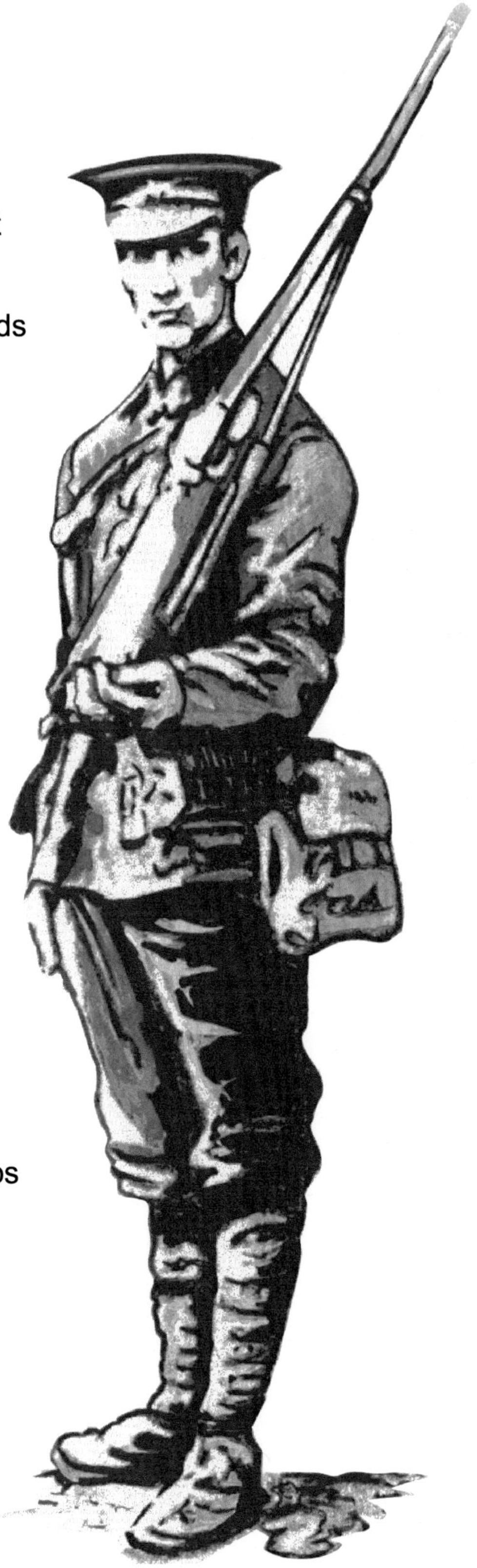

Hold them in your hearts
For they held Bramcote in theirs
Marching willingly to war
Whistling "Tipperary".

From mansion and cottage
Skilled men or gentleman's sons
Boarding troopships to Italy, Egypt
Flanders and France.

Bramcote men trudged duck-boards
Knew mud of the trenches
Bullets, screech of shells,
The madness of the Somme.

Had they visions of home,
The living green of Bluebell Hill
Before obliteration
In that shattered landscape?

Think of Charles Wilson
Midshipman - aged sixteen -
Dying on the "Bulwark"
Accidentally sunk in Sheerness.

Driver Harry Swift, forty,
Never saw the youngest
Of the four children
He left fatherless.

Remember the deep grief
Of the Pearsons, bereft
Of two sons: John in Egypt
Stephen on the Somme.

And Lieutenant Claye, Flying Corps
Forerunner of "The Few",
Whose frail craft thrust skies
One last time over France.

Amongst those known elsewhere
Old Bramcote names are listed-
Cooke, Cope, Eatch and Kirk,
Starbuck, Tomlinson-

Hold them all in your hearts
For they held Bramcote in theirs.

Sheila Town 2003

The Survivors

The Ex-Servicemen at the Opening of the Memorial Hall, 9th June 1923.

John Jesse Burton 17.11.1896 -
Gunner, Royal Field Artillery 92nd Brigade, Royal Field Artillery
Service Number 79936

Unknown child outside The Cottage.

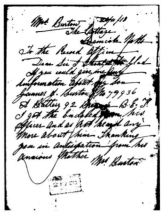

14th August 1917 The Revd. William Browne writes a letter to the army asking for news on behalf of Mrs. Burton.

John was born to Peter Henry Burton and his wife Mary Jane. He was baptised at Bramcote on 13th December 1896. John attended St. Michael's Sunday school being taught by Miss C. Smith. On 15th May 1909 John joined Beeston Boys' Brigade. The 1911 census sees him as a 14 year old gardener.

In March 1914 he joined the Territorial Force whilst working as a cycle hand at Raleigh. On 11th January 1915, stating that he was 19 years and 10 months old, John signed up with the Royal Field Artillery at Ilkeston. In fact he was only just 18 years old. He gives his occupation as a pipe tester, living at "The Cottage", Bramcote. He was sent to France on 24th July 1915 as a gunner.

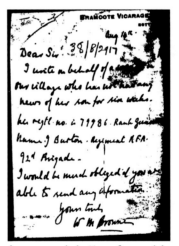

A second letter from his mother to the Record Office dated 24th November 1918 requesting information about her son.

John Jesse landed in France on 25th July 1915 with the original contingent of the 92nd Brigade, which at this point in the war was part of 20th Division. This Division took part in the Battle of Mount Sorrel and the Battle of the Somme 1916 which included the battles at Delville Wood, Guillemont, Flers-Courcelette, Morval and Le Transloy.

John was wounded on 6th November 1918 and on the 13th he was admitted to the General Hospital, Rouen, with a severe gunshot wound to his chest. A month later he was returned home to England. On 3rd April 1919 he was discharged from the army as being 30% disabled.

A family letter from 1922 says that John was living with his father Peter in Bramcote. He had a weekly pension of 8/- a week.

He is remembered by his great nephew as "the uncle with the metal plate in his chest."

Claude Chappell 23.7.1898 – 19.6.1969

Private, 6th Battalion, Army Cyclist Corps

Service Number 6244

Claude Chappell grew up in Bray Cottages, 35, Chapel Street, in the home of his grandparents, Charles and Ellen. The 1911 census return shows grandfather Charles was still working, at the age of 70, as a gardener in a nursery. Claude attended the Bramcote Church of England School and then began work at Raleigh in 1913.

Bray Cottages. Claude's home is on the left.

Two images of Claude as a young man

In later life, Claude must have looked back on his teenage years as being very different from the rest of his life. Having barely become accustomed to the workplace, he was soon to find himself serving his country on a bicycle. As Claude's war records do not appear to have survived, we can only generalise as to his role in the Army Cyclist Corps. Family members believe he served in France. He might have worked as a courier or as a scout or as part of a security patrol guarding French canals which were vulnerable to sabotage and patrolled by cyclists.

It was to a settled life in Bramcote that he was to return at the end of the conflict. Apart from the war years, Claude worked at Raleigh as a storekeeper from 1913 – 1963. A man of faith, he was confirmed in 1921 at St. Michael's and married Louie Harrison, a local girl and member of the choir, in the same church in 1925. In the 1930s he became the church verger and served conscientiously in this role for more than 30 years, becoming, as a result, a very well known local figure. At his funeral, following his sudden death in 1969, there were many tributes to "a man of loyalty, integrity and sincerity" who would be "greatly missed both from the parish church and from the village where he had spent all his life".

Claude as verger at St. Michael's Church

Long service award from Raleigh

Joseph Clifford 14.11.1888 – 7.3.1966
Sergeant, 14th Battalion York & Lancaster Regiment
Service Number 14/408

Herbert Clifford 10.12.1891 – 5.5.1967
Private, Army Service Corps (M.T.)
Service Number M2/167614

Joseph and Herbert Clifford were the two eldest sons of Charles and Eliza Clifford, who had seven children. In the census of 1901 the family were resident on Town Street but by 1911 they had moved to Cow Lane. There is a story that Charles Clifford was killed by being blown off a haystack at the bottom of Cow Lane as a result of the force of the explosion at Chilwell Munitions Factory in 1918.

Joseph Clifford

At the age of 12, Joseph was recorded on the family's census return as a carter on a farm but he was later to earn a living, like his father, as a miner. On the 28th March 1910 he married Nellie Gore, whose father was a baker and the couple went to live with Nellie's parents on Villa Street, Beeston. They had two children who were called in turn, Nellie and Joseph. Joseph's war records have not survived but his medal record card shows he enlisted on 2nd February 1915 and was discharged, having attained the rank of sergeant, on 17th August 1918.

Joe, Nellie and little Joe

Herbert Clifford

In the 1911 census, Herbert Clifford was recorded as a coal miner but at the time of his enlistment in the Army Service Corps, he gave his occupation as driver. Wonderful photographs exist of Herbert as a chauffeur delivering passengers to the Royal Hippodrome Nottingham.

Herbert is the chauffeur in the car on the left of this picture

Herbert attested at Beeston on 11th December 1915 but was not mobilised until 30th March 1916. In the interim he had married Ethel Cartwright at Beeston Parish Church. Her father had a confectionery shop at 44, Chilwell Road and the couple's home was initially above the shop.

Cartwright's confectionery shop, Chilwell Road

One of Wortley and Clifford's fleet of vehicles, delivering milk? on Church Street, Bramcote

Herbert's war records indicate that, following his initial departure from Southampton to Rouen, on 5th May 1916, he spent his war service as a driver attached to a number of motor transport companies undertaking different missions in France. On 19th December 1918, Herbert was given 7 days' leave and then had to report to the Discharge Centre at Ripon to be transferred to the reserve for the "the purpose of work in coal mines". Having escaped once from the pits, Herbert seems to have been determined not to descend again and went on to create a haulage business with a friend called Wortley. It is thought that this was Richard or Dick Wortley who had also lived on Cow Lane as a young man. Amongst other business they undertook was the delivery, in the late 1920s, of the two white lions, designed by Joseph Else, the head of the Nottingham School of Art, into the Council House Square in Nottingham. The business was successful and at the time of the nationalisation of road haulage in 1947, it was listed in the top 250 such businesses in the country.

In the 1930s Herbert and Ethel relocated to 64, Imperial Road, Beeston, where examples of World War One "trench art", such as polished spent 5 inch shells housing knitting needles, were on display in the parlour's fireplace. They had 5 children, though sadly one daughter did not survive infancy. Their second son, Harold, became well known locally as a councillor and the proprietor of a garage in Chilwell.

Eliza Clifford surrounded by her family in Henson Square in the 1920s. Joe is in the foreground on the right and Herbert is standing at the back, second from the right.

William Colville 10.5.1890 – 13.9.1966

Sergeant, 4th Suffolk Regiment
Service Number 5226; 202036

William was brought up by his grandparents, Richard and Mary Colville, on Town Street, Bramcote. Richard was a gardener from Strelley, who moved into his father-in-law's house after marrying Mary Ann Henson.

William's grandparents,
Richard and Mary Colville

William as a Boy

William attended the village school where he received a special prize at Christmas 1897 and he also gained an Easter prize from St. Michael's Sunday school in 1896. Both books are still in the possession of the Colville family.

William Colville enlisted with the Suffolk Regiment on 29th May 1915. He served on the Western Front with the 1/4th Suffolk Regiment , attaining the rank of sergeant. He was wounded, suffering a fractured arm, and was discharged on 27th April 1919. Records show that he was awarded the Silver War Badge for services rendered.

After the war, Bill, as he was known, worked, like his grandfather, as a gardener, being employed for many years by the Howitt family at Bramcote Grove. Today this is St. John's Theological College.

William in his army uniform

Whilst we have to rely on people's memories to discover what the returning soldiers did in their leisure time, there is some evidence that Bill Colville was a man who was "happy to have a go" at many things. He appears in photographs playing tennis, is pictured as a member of Bramcote football team and at his wedding there is a guard of honour with cricket bats held high, denoting some connection with Bramcote Cricket Club. He also took part in a number of local entertainments. A newspaper article from June 1920 reported his contribution to a play in the schoolroom where the aim was to raise funds for a war memorial. He also sang a solo and acted in a farce on the opening day of the Memorial Hall.

Bill married Alice Ann Smith, a local girl, in 1936. She was the daughter of Henry and Elizabeth Smith, who had 10 children, and lived at 169, Derby Road and then at Five Houses, also on Derby Road. The wedding was at St. Michael's and the reception was held in the Memorial Hall which was hired on 11th January 1936 for £1 from James Atkins, Kingston Garage.

William and Alice's wedding day

William and Alice
playing tennis at The Grove

William in the football team,
second from the left on the front row.

William and Alice had a son, Roger, who like his parents, spent many years as a chorister and regularly carried the cross at the head of the choir as it progressed. In fact it is as choristers at St. Michael's Church, Bramcote that both Bill and Alice are most affectionately recalled. Bill was a chorister for 47 years and Alice for 69 years and there are memorials to both of them in the church.

They lived at 17, Marshall Drive which they bought for £565 on 8th June 1936 from A.H.Marshall, The Firs, Starch Lane. A receipt for the purchase of an Anderson shelter in May 1947 for 15 shillings has also been found. Like many of their generation, they had to endure a second world war during which Bill served as a special constable.

John Cope 14.3.1876 - 6.7.1923

Gunner, Royal Garrison Artillery

Service Number 176686

John was born in Bramcote and brought up by his mother Martha and when she died in childbirth in 1880, by his stepfather, Charles Ruff. Later he was fostered by William and Emma Pollard of Town Street. On the 1881 census he was shown as John C. Ruff living on Cow Lane but by the 1891 census he was back to being John Cope living on Chapel Street. By 1901 he was working as a butler to Colonel Gardener late of the 11th Hussars at Newton Hall in Essex.

On 7th June 1905 he married Annie Roberts in Wales. At this time he was working as butler at Walworth Hall in Gloucestershire. The family moved to Bramcote in about 1910 and John became butler to Lieutenant Colonel Pearson of The White House, Bramcote. They lived at Rose Cottage Bramcote.

John attested at Ilkeston on 24th June 1916 but was not called up for service until 7th September 1917. He served on the Western Front with 504 Siege Battery, Royal Garrison Artillery from 15th February 1918. He was injured in June 1918 and sent back to hospital in Manchester in July. He was discharged, paralysed, on 20th September 1918 aged 42 years and spent the rest of his life in Ellerslie House, Nottingham. For his service he received a weekly pension of 21/6d. On his service record he is described as "A steady and hardworking man." He was awarded a Silver War Badge on his discharge for services rendered.

John Cope

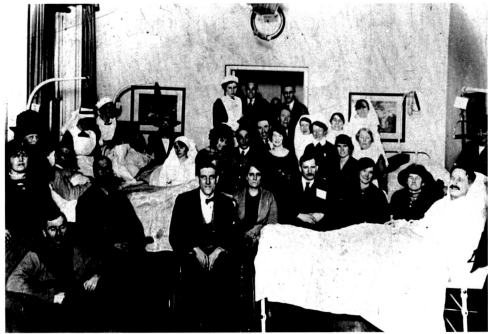

John Cope in bed, a patient at Ellerslie House

Ellerslie House on Gregory Boulevard was set up in 1917 to provide long term care for servicemen with back and other paralysing injuries. The building was purchased by the 6th Duke of Portland, and run by a committee. Any operations needed were performed at the General Hospital.

James Henry Daykin 1892 – 25.9.1963

Driver, 117th Battery, Royal Field Artillery

Service Number 106771

James was the eldest son of Joseph Daykin's 23 children from 2 marriages! Joseph was a miner born in Swinton, South Yorkshire and he married Kate Turton from Bilston, Staffordshire at St. Michael's, Bramcote on 27th August 1892. The 1901 census shows the Daykins and their 5 children in Chapel Street. By 1911 they were in Victoria House, a property set back from The White Lion, Town Street. Kate had died and Joseph was now married to Amy and there were 10 children. The last child of the 23 was born in 1926.

James Henry Daykin

Like his father, James was described as a miner when he enlisted in Nottingham on 9th August 1915. His papers show him to have been 5 feet and 3.75 inches tall. He joined the Royal Field Artillery at Newcastle-on-Tyne on 18th August and served for over 3 years in France.

On 2nd January 1919 he was given a posting to Harrowby Dispersal Camp, near Grantham for release as a miner and embarked from Dunkirk on 9th January 1919. He was formally demobbed from Woolwich on 8th February 1919.

Joseph and Kate Daykin with James, William, Ernest, Joseph and Annie

William, James and Harold Daykin
members of the Imperial Order of Oddfellows,
Middleton Lodge

As well as James three of his younger brothers, William Thomas, Joseph Clarence and Ernest Leslie, also served their country and survived the conflict.

Sarah and James Daykin

In 1923 James married Sarah Towlson and they set up home in a cottage above The White Lion, where today there is a modern bungalow. James worked at Trowell Pit until its closure and then at Beeston Boiler Company. He enjoyed sport and played cricket and football for the Bramcote teams. Along with some of his brothers, he was a member of the Middleton Lodge of The Imperial Order of Oddfellows. Sarah worked in Nottingham, in the hosiery trade, walking to Beeston to catch a train each day. They are both buried in St. Michael's churchyard.

Bilbie Exton c.1882 – 1961

Corporal, Royal Engineers
Service Number WR21555

Bilbie was born in Clifton, Nottingham. He went to work at Clifton Hall as a gardener and it was here he met his future wife, Maggie, who worked as a laundry maid. They married on 25th November 1906 and moved to Bramcote where Bilbie was employed as a gardener working for Mr. Poyser at Hall Gardens (this is where Harley House stands today). A house on Town Street went with the job. They had four children, Florence, Arthur, Walter and Eric. Maggie continued her laundry work for the Pearsons at The White House, the Smiths at Bramcote Hall and for the church. After the cottage was sold as part of the Holden Estate in 1919 the family moved next door to 36, Town Street, opposite The White Lion public house.

Bilbie attested at Beeston on 6th December 1915 and the following letters can be found in his service record.

> *"The War Office*
> *Director General of Military Railways*
>
> *Please enlist Mr. B. Exton in the Road Construction Companies, R.E., now being formed for service in France, provided he is medically fit for road making in that country......When his services are required he will be called up and should be given a railway warrant and instructed to report to the Officer Commanding, R.E. Railway Troops, Borden Camp, Hants. (L. & S.W. Railway), to whom his documents should be sent as soon as possible".*

> *"J. Cracroft Haller,*
> *County Surveyor,*
> *Shire Hall,*
> *Nottingham.*
> *12th December 1916*
>
> *I have now received instructions from the War Office asking you to report yourself to the Recruiting Officer at Ilkeston........you will be given instructions as to how to get to Borden Camp, where you will be placed in the company to which you will be attached for road work in France....."*

Bilbie Exton

He was mobilised a year later and went to France in February 1917, aged 35 years. His papers show that he mainly worked in the Boulogne area for the 331st Road Construction Company of the Waterways and Railways Battalion. He was promoted to corporal in January 1919 and it was not long before he was dispersed on 12th April from Harrowby Camp, Grantham.

Bilbie returned to his work as a gardener in Bramcote. In 1923 Mr. and Mrs Poyser, the Nottingham jewellers, gave Bilbie a watch for "his thought and skill in laying out the Hall Gardens." His grand-daughter, Hillary, remembers him as a man who loved the outdoors, taking her on walks around Bramcote and teaching her about the natural world. He was a rose grower and was often in demand as a judge, and was remembered around Bramcote for wearing a fresh rose in his buttonhole every weekend.

Bilbie and his dog Gyp and his son Arthur
(the child is Jackie Thorpe)

He was also a bell ringer, being master of the bells at St. Mary's Church, Clifton before his marriage. Family history says that when he moved to Bramcote and heard the bells at St. Michael's, he was in despair at the racket they made, so he went to see the vicar who said that if he could do better, he should get on with it. Thus began his long service at St. Michael's.

Bramcote Special Constables c.1939 - Bilbie is sitting 2nd left.

John Wilfred Headland 22.4.1897 – 19.4.1959

Private, Leicester Regiment

Service Number 17856

Wilf, as he was known, was the eldest son of William and Ada Headland and had three sisters and one brother. He was born and brought up at "The Hulks" off Coventry Lane, Bramcote. The 1919 Holden Estate sale document describes the family cottage as being at the side of the Radford and Trowell railway line. The cottage consisted of "a living room, lobby, dairy, 2 bedrooms and attic, wash-house, piggery and earth closet, together with garden plot." His father William was a canal bank labourer, and walked to Hucknall every day for his work. Wilf attended Bramcote Church of England School and later became an ironworker.

He enlisted at Ilkeston on 15th April 1915 aged 17 years, although his attestation papers show him as 19 years old. He embarked for France on 18th August 1915 where he became a machine gunner.

He had a stay in hospital from September to December 1916 suffering from shell shock, and after returning to the front he was then injured by shrapnel in his left thigh. He was admitted to hospital on 11th May 1917, and then invalided to England a week later, where he was admitted to the 4th London General Hospital, Denmark Hill. He stayed there for 149 days, and didn't talk or communicate for much of that time from the shock of what had happened. He suffered pain on walking and standing for any length of time, and on 22nd September he was recommended for discharge from the army which took place on 15th October 1917. He was awarded the Silver War Badge on his discharge.

John Wilfred Headland

Wilf and Gertie and their families

He went to work for Judge Allen at Southfield House, Common Lane as a gardener and met his future wife Gertrude Jackson who was in service. They remembered Judge Allen as a "good boss."

Wilf and Gertrude were married at Lincoln on 21st December 1918. They went to live at Beeston, where Wilf was employed at the Ericsson Telephone Works as a tool setter. He had to retire in 1947 as he was unable to stand for any length of time.

Bernard John Mellor 1888 - 1955

Shoeing Smith, 243 Company Army Service Corps.
Service number TS/1490

Bernard John was the son of John and Sarah Mellor. In 1893, trade directories show that John was the blacksmith in Bramcote. On the 1911 census the family of five sons and one daughter, who were all born in Bramcote, were living at The Forge. Bernard took up his father's trade and is also shown as a blacksmith on the census with his younger brother William a blacksmith's striker.

An early recruit to the forces, Bernard enlisted into the Army Service Corps in Nottingham as a driver on 23rd November 1914, a single man describing his trade as a shoeing smith. His father provided a statement the following day explaining that the war had already caused a shortage of work in the forge and that his son had left his employment as a result. Already a skilled man he was posted to the Horse Transport.

Unfortunately details of his time in the army are scant but it is known that Bernard married during his war service. On 29th September 1916 he and Charlotte Ellen Black took their vows in Boston, Lincolnshire with the marriage recorded on his army form A.22 which gives his rank as "shoeing smith".

On 8th August 1917 he was sent to France and continued in service until he was demobilized at Woolwich Dockyard on the 27th June 1919 aged 30 years. His rank upon discharge was again shown as "shoe smith" and he was issued with his protection certificate in Ripon, Yorkshire on 30th May 1919. At this time his medical category was given as "A1" and he had a certificate confirming that he had no disability due to his military service. Bernard was then able to return to his wife Charlotte living in James Street, Boston, Lincolnshire.

William Boden Mellor 1889 - 1966

Shoeing Smith, Royal Field Artillery,
Service number 90129

William Boden Mellor, was a younger brother of Bernard. By the outbreak of war, William was a married man having wed in May 1913. Subsequently, he, his wife Kate and baby daughter moved to Radford, where they were living when William enlisted into the Army on 20th March 1915. Like his brother, William joined the Army Service Corps and spent his first eighteen months as a shoe smith later serving with the Royal Field Artillery. He served for a total of three years and thirty-three days, mainly in France, and was transferred to the Army Reserve on 15th January 1919 when his health was, like his brother, shown as "A1".

William and Kate had eight children and were known to have been living on Moorbridge Lane in Stapleford in 1920. They also lived in a pit house at the top of the lane leading down to Shipley Colliery.

The Smithy and Forge

Noel Gervis Pearson 30.9.1884 – 26.11.1958
Lieutenant Colonel, 2/16th (London Regiment)
Queen's Westminster Rifles

Noel Gervis was the youngest son of Henry John Pearson and his wife Laura, and he, like his brothers was born in Beeston, later moving to The White House in Bramcote. Noel, known as "Gervis", was educated at Charterhouse School and studied engineering at Nottingham University College. He later gained practical engineering experience in Nottingham and the United States of America. Like his brother Hetley he later became a director and then chairman of the family run Beeston Foundry Company.

Gervis married Kathleen Mary Nicholls on 18th June 1913 and between the years of 1914 and 1924 the couple had four sons, two of whom were twins, and two daughters. Following the deaths of both his father and older brother Hetley, Gervis and his family continued to live at The White House.

The White House

Like his older twin brothers, Gervis enlisted into the army. One of the first volunteers in August 1914, he joined the 9th Sherwood Foresters and was commissioned from the ranks on 23rd November 1914 as 2nd Lieutenant. Gervis was sent to the Western Front in August 1915 by which time he was serving as Captain and Adjutant with the 12th Sherwood Foresters. He remained on active service until March 1919. During this time he served as an Intelligence Officer with the 17th Infantry Brigade staff and as a Major in the 6th South Wales Borderers (Pioneers). In September 1918 he was given command of the 2/16th (London Regiment) Queen's Westminster Rifles.

He became the most decorated of the men associated with Bramcote having been awarded the M.C. in 1916 Birthday Honours, the D.S.O. in 1918 (for service at the Ploegstreet attack on the Germans) and having been twice mentioned in dispatches.

The London Gazette Supplement of 16th September 1918 printed the following D.S.O. citation:

"For conspicuous gallantry and devotion to duty in organising several minor counter-attacks and in carrying out many daring reconnaissances by night, when he invariably brought back valuable information. His cheerful spirit and courageous example inspired great confidence in all on many critical occasions".

Following his retirement from the army Colonel Pearson, as he was generally known, was a Lay Reader who took services in all parts of the Diocese of Southwell and also lead a very full life of public achievement. Generous with both his time and money, making many donations anonymously, he was highly active in service to hospitals.He was president or chairman

Lieutenant Colonel N. G. Pearson
D.S.O., M.C. in 1935

of the Nottingham Children's Hospital, the Nottingham General Hospital and the Nottingham General Dispensary. In addition he was chairman of the Nottingham No.1 Hospital Management Committee which governed many more Nottinghamshire hospitals. His interest in these hospitals extended to personal visits to the staff and wards and the broadcasting of prayers from the hospital chapel.

Colonel Pearson also took a direct interest in the British Legion (Beeston branch) of which he was a lifelong member. Like his brother Stephen he was also interested in the welfare of young people, becoming president of the Boys' Brigade in Beeston (17th Nottingham) and the Nottinghamshire County Commissioner of the Boy Scouts/Girl Guides. In 1935 he was appointed to the position of High Sheriff of Nottinghamshire.

During World War Two, two of his sons, Pilot Officer Henry Hetley and Lieutenant Basil John Pearson, were to lose their lives in the service of their country.

Noel Gervis Pearson died at his home in Bramcote on 26th November 1958 aged 74, one year after the death of his wife Kathleen. In his will he left the University of Nottingham a significant collection of birds and birds' eggs assembled by his father, who was a keen ornithologist, and also made generous bequests to the Nottingham No. 1 Hospital Management Committee, the Nottingham Boy Scouts Association and the Southwell Diocesan Board of Finance. Colonel Pearson was the last member of the family living in Bramcote, therefore after his death, "The White House" was sold.

Elijah Tagg 1885 – 16.5.1946

Private, Army Ordnance Corps

Service Number 040458

Born in Linby, Elijah lived in Trowell as a child and then worked as a labourer on a farm in Wollaton. He married Annie Hewitt in 1910 and appears on the 1911 census with her and a daughter, Grace, living on Cow Lane, Bramcote. He is working as a miner at this time. Annie is not working but was recorded as a cigarette packer in the previous census of 1901.

Elijah Tagg

Elijah went to France in March 1915 with the 4th King's Royal Rifle Corps. He was wounded during the 2nd Battle of Ypres in late April 1915; the family believe that he was shot. On his recovery, he was transferred to the Army Ordnance Corps where he would have been concerned with the supply and maintenance of weaponry and equipment.

Wedding party on path at 21, Cow Lane
following the marriage of Grace Tagg and Ivan Brelsford. Elijah can be seen back right.

Post war, Elijah resumed his colliery work and is known to have been at Radford Pit. He paid a subscription to the Bramcote Cricket Club in 1919 and in later life enjoyed playing dominoes at The White Lion. Elijah and Annie had six children but sadly two of them died as infants. At the time of his death in 1946, Elijah was living at 21, Cow Lane.

Those remembered in
St. Michael's Churchyard, Bramcote.

Bertie Croft and William Harris who served during World War One are buried in the churchyard, but not listed on the memorial within the church. Charles Wilson is remembered on his father's gravestone.

Bertie Croft 1894 - 23.4.1918

Private, 7th Battalion Suffolk Regiment
Service Number 43044

Private Bertie Croft of Bramfield, Suffolk appears to have been a horse dealer at the outbreak of World War One. He enlisted on 1st October 1914, aged 19 years and served for 3 years and 102 days, mainly in France.

On 28th April 1917, at Monchy, he suffered shrapnel wounds to his back and abdomen and was declared unfit for further service following a medical examination in Manchester on 20th December 1917. He was formally discharged on 10th January 1918 with a Silver War Badge and at this time he was described as being a labourer living near Wickham Market in Suffolk.

He died of his wounds on St. George's Day, 23rd April 1918 and he was buried in St. Michael's churchyard, Bramcote on 26th April. The Reverend Walter Marshall Browne's note alongside Bertie's entry in the burial book explains why this Suffolk man came to be interred here. His death had occurred whilst employed at the Chilwell Munitions Works and he had been lodging in Bramcote, though there is no record of his temporary address.

William Henry Harris 1876 – 6.2.1920

Private, Labour Corps
Service Number 292125

Born in the late 1870s in the USA, though his exact date of birth and place of origin are unknown, William Harris grew up in the South Derbyshire area and was a British citizen. His father, Thomas, was described as a widowed tailor from Nottingham in the 1891 census so quite how he came to be born in the U.S.A. is something of a mystery. By 1901 he had married Rose from Smethwick and they had a two roomed home in Sheffield. Sadly a decade later the census recorded that William was a widower, earning his living as a cinder crusher at Stanton Ironworks and living with his three daughters, Edith, Margaret and Sarah Jane in Little Hallam Lane, Ilkeston By the outbreak of World War One, he was living at Ladycroft Cottage in Sandiacre with his second wife, Catherine Harriett, whom he had married on 22nd March 1914 in Sandiacre. Their marriage certificate reveals that they had both been widowed.

On 19th August 1915 in London, William joined the Royal Engineers but after being gassed, he was transferred, in 1917, to the Labour Corps. Most of his three years and two hundred and forty two days of warfare were spent in France. He was discharged in April 1919, with a Silver War Badge, being no longer deemed fit for service and joined his wife, Catherine, whose maiden name had been Whittlesee and who had been born in Bramcote, in a property on Chapel Street. William suffered greatly from ill-health over the next few months and he died on 6th February 1920. The cause of death was recorded as heart disease, attributed to the effects of being gassed.

Ladycroft Cottage

A very impressive military funeral took place in Bramcote. A contingent of the 51st Battalion Gordon Highlanders, including a firing party, pipe band and bearers, came from the Clipstone Camp, Mansfield in order to honour this ex-serviceman. The Sandiacre and Stapleford Weekly News of 13th February 1920 described the solemn occasion:

"As the coffin covered with the Union Jack was borne into the street, the firing party reversed arms, then slowly marched up the street leading the way to the parish church. Behind the firing party, the band with draped drums fell in ...... the band played plaintive, mournful music .... The firing party fired three volleys over the grave, during which time the pipe major played soul-moving strains by the open grave. Then the bugler sounded "The Last Post"."

There is a Commonwealth War Graves Commission memorial to William Harris in St. Michael's Churchyard.

Charles Huband Wilson c.1898 - 26.11.1914
Midshipman, Royal Navy

Charles Wilson had the misfortune to serve on the ill-fated battleship HMS Bulwark. This 15,000 ton vessel was launched in October 1889,but suffered several mishaps culminating in its demise on Thursday 26th November 1914. Having sailed into Sheerness Harbour, the Bulwark was taking aboard ammunition when an explosion occurred that lit the sky for some 20 miles around.

HMS Bulwark

This was initially thought to be the work of an enemy saboteur but, following an official investigation, it was revealed that the explosion was due to a 12 inch shell detonating, whilst being loaded into the fore magazine. It was all over in three minutes, leaving only 14 survivors from a complement of 726.

Midshipman Wilson died on that day, aged just 16 years and is remembered on the Portsmouth Naval Memorial, Southsea (panel1).

Portsmouth Naval Memorial. Photograph courtesy of Commonwealth War Graves Commission. (www.cwgc.org)

Wilson family grave in St. Michael's Churchyard

His connection with Bramcote is tenuous ---
he probably never lived in the village but he is remembered on his father's gravestone in St. Michael's churchyard. The latter was Charles John Wilson, husband of Jane Mary Wilson, who resided originally at Derlamogue, Allesbury Park, Dublin but was buried in Bramcote following his death in 1955, aged 80.

Men from the parish who served in WW1 and returned

1. The Absentee Voters' List on the Electoral Registers 1918 & 1919
2. The Soldiers' Prayer List from the Church Parish Magazine dated 1916

Name	Address	Service Details	1	2
Ainger William Fred	Unknown	62762 Bombardier, Royal Field Artillery (later Corporal)		*
Appleton Frank	Derby Road	19938 Sergeant, 3rd Reserve Battalion, King's Own Yorkshire Light Infantry	*	*
Bexon William	Moved to Beeston	8th Sherwood Foresters		*
Birkin Philip Austin	The Grove	Major, Reserve of Officers	*	
Blake Charles	Town Street	435902 Private, Labour Corps	*	
Broomfield William	Unknown	Royal Engineers		*
Burton John Jesse	Town Street	77936 Private, A Battery 92nd Brigade, Royal Field Artillery	*	*
Campbell Arthur	Unknown	Lieutenant, 7th (Robin Hood) Sherwood Foresters		*
Chappell Claude	Chapel Street	6244 Private, 6th Cyclist Battalion, Army Cyclist Corps	*	*
Chappell Leonard	Chapel Street	34016 Private, Royal Army Medical Corps	*	*
Chilvers Charles Ernest	Chapel Street	63223 Private, 165th Company, Royal Defence Corps	*	
Clarke Albert	Chapel Street	1st Sherwood Foresters	*	*
Clarke Thomas	Chapel Street	2nd Lieutenant, Tank Corps (had been Lance Corporal in Cameronians)	*	*
Clifford Herbert	Cow Lane	Private M2/167614 Army Service Corps		
Clifford Joseph	Had moved to Beeston	14/408 Sergeant, 14th York and Lancaster Regiment		*
Colville William	Town Street	202036 Sergeant, 4th Suffolk Regiment	*	*
Congreave George	Town Street	306391 (also 4284 & 59053)Private, 8th Sherwood Foresters		*
Cooke Ernest James	Cow Lane	M2/181343 Private, 955th Motor Transport Company, Army Service Corps	*	
Cooke James	Town Street	4/105553 Private, 4th Sherwood Foresters	*	
Cooke Harold	Town Street	14122 Gunner, 124th Battery 28th Brigade, Royal Field Artillery	*	*
Cope Arthur	Church Street	34334 Bombardier, A Battery 256th Brigade, Royal Field Artillery	*	*
Cope John	Rose Cottage Town Street	176686 Private, 504 Siege Battery, Royal Garrison Artillery	*	
Cope John	Church Street	141181 Driver, D Battery 64th Brigade, Royal Field Artillery	*	
Cope (John)Thomas	Church Street	4417 Trooper, 2nd Life Guards	*	*
Cross Arthur J	Unknown	338 & 612025 Bombardier, Nottinghamshire Royal Horse Artillery		*
Cross Joseph	Town Street	35614 Driver, A Battery 106th Brigade, Royal Field Artillery	*	*
Daykin Ernest Leslie	Victoria House Town Street	59053 Private, West Yorkshire Regiment	*	
Daykin James Henry	Victoria House Town Street	106771 Driver, Royal Field Artillery	*	*
Daykin Joseph Clarence	Victoria House Town Street	270387 Driver, 3rd Battery, Royal Field Artillery	*	
Daykin Joseph Henry	Victoria House Town Street	York and Lancaster Regiment		*
Daykin William Thomas	Victoria House Town Street	270284 Gunner, No. 2 Reserve Brigade Artillery, Territorial Force	*	

Dunford Arthur	Town Street	226580 Motor Transport, Army Service Corps	*	
Edwards Joseph	Unknown	7th (Robin Hood) Sherwood Foresters		*
Ellis Arthur	Unknown	15th Sherwood Foresters		*
Exton Bilbie	Town Street	WR/21555 Corporal, 308th Road Construction Company, Royal Engineers	*	
Griffiths James	Unknown	7th (Robin Hood) Sherwood Foresters		*
Harris William Henry	Chapel Street	292125 Private, 704th Company Labour Corps	*	
Headland John Wilfred	Coventry Lane	17856 Private, 8th Leicester Regiment		*
Hewitt George	Town Street	A/1154 (S) Gunner, Royal Marines, H.M.S. "Royal Oak"	*	*
Hewitt Joshua	Town Street	23971 Lance Corporal, 2nd Grenadier Guards	*	*
Holden Ernest Frank	Bramcote Hill	Major, Reserve of Officers	*	
Hunt Ernest Alfred	The Manse Church Street	306250 Private, Sherwood Foresters, transferred to Lincolnshire Regiment 63909	*	
Husbands John	Chapel Street	820295 Gunner, 46th Division, Royal Field Artillery	*	
Husbands Frank	Chapel Street	241605 Gunner, 123rd Battery, 28th Brigade Royal Field Artillery	*	
Hutchby John	Town Street	206171 Lance Corporal, 2/6th Sherwood Foresters, transferred to Labour Corps 657668	*	
Jackson Cecil George	Derby Road	60041 Private, 21st Battalion, Machine Gun Corps	*	
Kidger Frederick	Chapel Street	243058 Private, 9th King's Own Yorkshire Light Infantry	*	
Layte Robert	Chapel Street	59591 Gunner, 331st Siege Battery, Royal Garrison Artillery	*	
Lees Albert Edward	Bramcote Moor	T/327926 Private, 49th Reserve Supply Depot, Army Service Corps	*	
Marshall Robert	Unknown	Army Service Corps		*
Martin Harold	Church Street (previously Reine Cottage Town Street)	275351 Private, 1st Garrison Battalion, Somerset Light Infantry (had been in 6th Royal Sussex)	*	*
Martin Sidney	Unknown	14635 8th Sherwood Foresters		*
Mellor Bernard John	The Smithy, Town Street	TS/1490 Driver, 243 Company, Army Service Corps, later Royal Horse Artillery		*
Mellor William Boden	The Smithy, Town Street	90129 Shoeing Smith, Army Service Corps, later Royal Field Artillery		*
Mellors James	Town Street	33158 Private, Royal Army Medical Corps, Woking	*	*
Peachy Harry	Church Street	44111 Private, Essex Regiment	*	
Peachy John Thomas	Church Street	89958 Private, Royal Army Medical Corps, Woking	*	*
Pearson Noel Gervis	The White House	Lieutenant Colonel, 2/16th London Regiment (had been Captain 12th Sherwood Foresters)	*	*
Pepper Harold	Chapel Street	43146 Private, 7th Lincolnshire Regiment had been 22260 9th Sherwood Foresters.	*	*
Sharp William	Church Street	270358 Gunner, 60th (later 53rd)Reserve Battery, Royal Field Artillery	*	
Shaw Cyril	Cow Lane	16780 Sergeant, 4th Scottish Rifles (had been Lance Corporal 9th Scottish Rifles)	*	*

Shepherd Ernest Herbert George	Chapel Street	175584 Gunner, 484th Siege Battery, Royal Garrison Artillery	*	
Short Charles William	Unknown	17658 7th South Staffordshire Regiment		*
Simpkins George	Town Street	2737 Corporal, 24th Royal Fusiliers	*	*
Smith Evelyn Kyrle	Bramcote Hall	Lieutenant, Royal Naval Volunteer Reserve "President V"	*	
Swift George	In Canada	147676 78th Battalion (Winnipeg Grenadiers) Canadian Expeditionary Force		*
Tagg Elijah	Philo House Cow Lane	R10471 Private, King's Royal Rifles	*	*
Tolson Frederick	Ilkeston Road	M2/032219 Quarter Masters Stores, Motor Transport, Army Service Corps	*	*
Tomlinson Jesse	Town Street	22050 Private, 3rd Battalion, Grenadier Guards	*	*
Towlson Arthur	Town Street	R10472 Private King's Royal Rifles		*
Walker Edwin	White Lion Town Street	63969 Private, 15th South Lancashire, No. 9 Company	*	
Webber Arthur	Bankfield Farm	239673 Private, Agric Battalion, Logistics Corps	*	
Wright Wilfred	Unknown	Medical Unit, Royal Naval Division		*

Some of the men who were remembered on the prayer list in 1916 appear to have moved away by the time the absentee voters' list was published in 1918.

Bramcote Memorial Hall

Opening Day, 9th June 1923

Bramcote Memorial Hall

Bramcote Parish Council held a meeting on 12th May 1919 inviting parishioners to consider what form the parish war memorial should take. At this meeting it was decided that the best way to commemorate the sacrifices of The Great War was the erection of an institute in which should be placed a list of the Bramcote men who had served their country and a list of those who had fallen[1]. The Parish Council then set up a committee to oversee this project.

Council Members:

The Revd. W. M. Browne
Mr. Henson
Major Holden
Plus:
Mr. Dowson
Mr. Woodward

The following additional village residents were added to the committee:

Mrs. Holden
Col. N. G. Pearson
Mr. Birkin
Mr. G. Adcock
Mr. C. Chappell
Miss M. P. Enfield
Mr. J. Daykin
Dr. & Mrs. Buckley
Mr. A. Towlson
Mr. J. Simpkin.

Funds were raised, land was purchased and The Memorial Hall which stands on Church Street in Bramcote was designed and built. It was formally opened in a ceremony on Saturday 9th June 1923.

A social committee did sterling work with fund-raising activities and there were a number of generous benefactors including Lt. Col. Noel Gervis Pearson, his mother, Laura Kate Pearson and The Miners' Welfare Fund which gave £150.

[1] The list of those who had fallen was actually placed in the Parish Church.

Trustees of the War Memorial Fund

By 1922 substantial funds had been raised and on 13th March 1922 the Parish Council appointed five trustees to bring the plans to fruition:-

1. Mr. Frank Henson.

Chairman of the Parish Council and a J.P., Frank would have brought pertinent knowledge to this assignment as he was a carpenter and joiner. He lived at a house called "Netherdale" on Town Street.

2. Mr. Henry Houghton Enfield

Henry was the Treasurer of the Parish Council. He had been educated at Trinity College, Cambridge and was a solicitor in the family firm on Low Pavement as well as being President of the Nottingham Law Society in 1913. He was also a trustee of the almshouses. He lived at The Grange at the top of Town Street.

3. Lt. Col. Noel Gervis Pearson D.S.O., M.C.

Whilst Lt. Col. Pearson was a decorated war hero, he had also experienced the anguish of losing his twin brothers, Stephen and John, in the war. He would have expertise of running operations, not just from his military background but also as a director of Beeston Foundry Company (later Beeston Boiler Company). He lived in The White House at the top of Town Street, which is now a nursing home.

4. Mr. Arthur Towlson

It might be that local folk thought that Arthur was their real representative in this venture. Like so many others, he was a miner who had given years of his life to serve his country, returning thankfully in good health to this village where he went on to be the church verger.

5. The Reverend Walter Marshall Browne

A Cambridge graduate in history and theology, Walter was very much a "man of the people" from the time he arrived in Bramcote in 1916. He spent time with grieving families and would have seen the need for a permanent memorial. He also seems to have been an energetic man and this would have been a major project for Bramcote village.

Mr. Stanley Briggs was appointed Secretary of the Memorial Fund for Bramcote.

The Site

On 19th June 1922, 880 square yards of land with a 28 yards frontage to Church Street was conveyed to the Memorial Hall Trustees for £110 by William Lowe. (Details from the Bramcote Memorial Hall Trust Deed)

Church Street pre-Memorial Hall

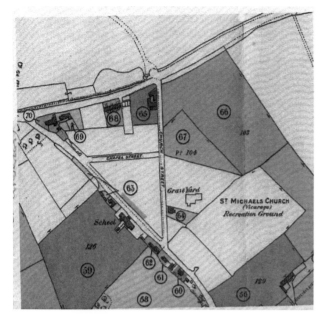

This is a section of the map from the 1919 sale showing Bramcote Memorial Hall land (lot 67). There are many other Bramcote properties that are still standing eg: Ivy House was lot 65.

This land was part of Lot 67 purchased by William Lowe at a sale on 28th May 1919 held at The Welbeck Hotel in Nottingham. Major Ernest Frank Holden offered at auction, in 69 separate lots, 920 acres of his estate in Bramcote and Stapleford. William Lowe was a well-known nurseryman who in the 1911 census was living at Hallaton House, Wollaton Road, Beeston and was the purchaser of several lots at the auction.

The land was originally farmland belonging to John Sherwin, the 19th century squire of Bramcote Hills. The estate had passed down the Holden family line to Ernest Frank, following the demise of his elder brothers. Frank Holden, as he was known, was an officer in the 5th Dragoon Guards and retired from the army in 1911. He was appointed M.B.E. in 1919 for his services in connection with the Nottingham Volunteer Corps.

Bramcote Hills House

The Building

The Memorial Hall plans were drawn up by Mr. C. F. Wilde, a Nottingham architect and were approved by Stapleford Rural District Council on 6th November 1922. Alterations to these plans to include a stage and dressing room were approved by the council on 29th January 1923.

The Pearson family were generous benefactors in Bramcote and it was fitting that the foundation stone was laid by Lt. Col. N. G. Pearson on 3rd February 1923 with what seems a cryptic message:

'THIS STONE WAS LAID BY
N.G.P.
FEB 3RD 1923
FOR H.J. & L.K.P.'

In full it would read, 'This stone was laid by Noel Gervis Pearson, February 3rd 1923, for his parents Henry John Pearson (1850-1913) and Laura Kate Pearson (1855-1938)'.

Building work was undertaken by Messrs. F. Perks and Sons Ltd., of Long Eaton. When finished the main hall could accommodate 250 people and had a splendid stage and The hall was equipped with the latest electric lighting and central heating! The cost including the land was approximately £1,800. The funds raised covered these costs so the Memorial Hall opened free of debt.

Opening Day Celebration 9th June 1923

This must have been an exciting, yet solemn, day in Bramcote's history when all the village folk would have gathered to participate in the proceedings as the new Memorial Hall was formally opened. The photographs suggest that the weather was fine and that all the surviving ex-servicemen were honoured alongside those whose lives were commemorated by the erection of this village facility.

Capt. Vickers V.C. with Dr. J. C. Buckley and The Revd. W. M. Browne in front of the Memorial Hall doors. The buglers are from the Boys' Brigade and veterans can be seen proudly wearing their medals.

A Special Guest

The opening ceremony was performed by Capt. G. Vickers V.C. who had served in The Sherwood Foresters. As well as being a Nottinghamshire war hero, Capt. Vickers had a connection directly with Bramcote as he was the brother-in-law of the vicar, The Reverend. Walter Marshall Browne. Captain Vickers was awarded the V.C. for action on 14th October 1915 at the Hohenzollern redoubt during the Battle of Loos. He was seriously wounded but recovered sufficiently to receive his medal at Buckingham Palace in January 1916. In 1918 he was further awarded the Belgian Croix de Guerre for his actions when in command of a battalion at the Second Battle of the Marne.

Captain G. Vickers V.C.

(In peacetime he became a solicitor and during the Second World War served as Deputy Director General in the Ministry of Economic Warfare, specialising in economic intelligence).

Details of the day's proceedings were carefully recorded in The Sandiacre and Stapleford News of 16th June 1923. Some attendees, notably many ladies, are specifically named. They are listed here together with the names of their homes:

Mrs. Browne, *(The Vicarage).*

Mrs. Pearson, *(The White House).*

Mrs. Hardy, *(Bramcote Hills House).*

Miss M. Enfield, *(The Grange).*

Miss Birkin, *(The Grove).*

Mrs. Buckley, *(Southfields House).*

Other attendees were :

Mr. and Mrs. B. W. Grainger (Beeston), Mr. G. Anstee Perks (Long Eaton), Councillor F. Henson, Mr. and Mrs. F. Peel, Mr. G. A. Jackson (Secretary of the Building Committee) and Mr. Thomas (Secretary of the Social Committee). The local ex-servicemen wearing their medals, Girl Guides (under Miss Birkin and Miss Critchlow), and Wolf Cubs were lined up in front of the hall.

The proceedings

The vicar first offered prayer and then read the names of the men from Bramcote who made the supreme sacrifice as follows:-

Lieut. R. L. B. Allen, *R.F.A.*

Capt. H. B. Bartram, *R.H.A.*

Pte. A. H. Burton, *South Staffs.*

Lieut. C. G. Claye, *R.F.C.*

Pte. G. Cooke, *Scottish Rifles*

Pte. E. Eatch, *Lancs. Fusiliers*

Pte. R. Hallam, *Notts. and Derbys.*

Cpl. F. Kirk, *Notts. and Derbys.*

Pte. C. Lavelle, *Machine Gun Corps*

Cpl. J. S. Pearson, *New Zealand Machine Gun Corps*

Sec-Lieut. S. H. Pearson, *Grenadier Guards*

Pte. J. Starbuck, *South Notts. Hussars*

Pte. H. Swift, *R.E.*

Gunner A. Thorpe, *R.F.A.*

Pte. H. Tomlinson, *Grenadier Guards*

Buglers then sounded "The Last Post".

The first address was delivered by Dr. J. C. Buckley of Southfields House, who chaired the proceedings. Initially a general practitioner, Dr. Buckley went on to be a consultant physician at Nottingham General Hospital. Dr. Buckley had served on the committee that developed the Memorial Hall project.

Dr. J. C. Buckley

Dr. Buckley spoke of the sacrifices made by the fallen and referred to the Memorial Hall as "an outward visible sign or acknowledgement of the great services rendered by the gallant band of heroes who at the sound of a drum left the little village and went forth to play the part of men in the cause of right and justice. It was fitting that the person with whom lay the honour of opening the building was a gallant gentleman who had shared the vicissitudes of the lads and had been decorated with the highest military honour in the land. The deeds of the Bramcote lads WOULD NEVER be forgotten by the Bramcote people." The speaker acknowledged the generous interest and support received in connection with the project from the late Mr. Henry Pearson and Mrs. Laura Kate Pearson and their son Lt. Col. Pearson, The Miners' Welfare Fund, the Building Committee under Mr. Lindsay, the Social Committee, and Mr. C. F. Wilde, the architect. Dr. Buckley urged that their service to the lads should not end in the opening of the building, and concluded:

"Never must there be a repetition of those circumstances which led us to the catastrophe of 1914. Our duty is to do what we can to see that strife is no more."

Captain Vickers then unveiled a memorial stone over the entrance bearing the simple inscription, "Lest we forget, 1914-1918". In the course of his speech he said,

Tablet unveiled by Capt. Vickers V.C.

"During the war this nation was organised for service. It was a nation of servants. Those of us who came back forget. We talk about our rights. The curious theory arose that what any man had given his country he was entitled to be paid for, with interest if possible, in cash from the Germans or the Government or somebody. The dead did not come back.

They gave and passed on, and to those who died giving death gave a completeness that few can share. It is the fashion in these days to make the war our scapegoat. We lay upon its head everything from high prices to low spirits, from juvenile crime to adult scepticism. It is well to look back across four years of peace to four years of war and remember how much 'loyalty' and self-sacrifice went to winning the war, and let us not forget that for four years at least we worked as one for a cause greater than ourselves. We found in war a larger loyalty which we have not found in peace. I believe it can be found. I believe it must be found, and that it is for those who came back to find it. I believe that war will continue until it is found. Statistics will not stop war. Men are not moved by fear, and if this memorial stood for statistics alone, its significance would perish with the generation that built it. But it does not stand for statistics alone, and what better memorial to the dead could be raised than one to give a more abundant life to those whose liberties they guarded and for whom they died. A memorial is not a tombstone but a signpost. It is a light from the past shining to the future. It is my privilege to open a memorial of the past, but it is the privilege of you all to make it a beacon not of warning, but of guidance for the years to come."

Mr. F. Peel proposed a vote of thanks to the Chairman, Dr. Buckley, and Capt. Vickers which was heartily accorded.

Further events

After inspecting the interior of the building, the principal guests, by kind invitation of Mr. Eben Hardy of Bramcote Hills, were invited to his gardens to admire the fine display of rhododendrons. At 4pm, the ex-servicemen and other villagers were entertained to tea arranged by the Ladies' Committee in the new hall.

The Evening Concert

We can imagine that this would have been very well-attended as so many local folk were participating and everyone would want to see the various acts that were on offer. In the course of fund raising for the hall, similar sorts of entertainment appear to have been popular.

The Programme:

Part I

1. *Overture:* Simpkins' Trio

2. *'The Terrible Three':* Bramcote Cubs

3. *Song:* Miss L. Harrison

4. *Sword Dance (Haxby):* Girl Guides

5. *Song:* Mr. W. Colville

6. *Monologue:* Mr. J.B. Blaney

7. *Song:* Mr. F. Peel

8. *Some Prestidigitation:* Mr. Arch Doughty

9. *Song 'Kalua':* Miss E. Birkin

10. *Sketch 'Sacked':* Girl Guides

Interval

The Sandiacre and Stapleford News reported that the hall was packed and that the audience thoroughly appreciated the performers' efforts.

Registration as a charity

On 26th September 1923 a charity known as Bramcote Village Hall was founded by deed poll. (Bramcote Village Hall was conceived as a memorial to those who fell in World War One and is commonly known as Bramcote Memorial Hall, a reminder of why it was built).

An application was made on 9th November 1923 to the Charity Commissioners, by Henry Houghton Enfield and Frank Henson, to register Bramcote Village Hall as a charity. This was granted on 15th February 1924.

Part II

11. *Instrumental Selections:* Simpkins' Trio
12. *Selection:* Mr. J.B. Bradley
13. *Playlet:* 'Fanchette From France':
Girl Guides
Scene: Nursery Time
Midnight Characters: Dolls
14. *Wireless Selections:*
Messrs. S. Briggs & C. Chappell
15. *Pianoforte Selection*: Mr. L. Bowler
16. *'Uncle John From Yorkshire'*,
A Farce by Harry Taudi

Cast
Uncle John: Mr. W. Colville
Mr. Villiers: Mr. A. Towlson
Mrs. Villiers: Miss L. Harrison
Mary (the Maid): Miss E. Simpkin
Joseph (Butler): Mr. F. Ward

'God Save The King'

Purchase of Further Land

On 24th August 1925 a further 2,614 square yards of the land from Lot 67 purchased by William Lowe from Frank Holden was conveyed to the Memorial Hall Trustees for £201, including legal costs, to form the Memorial Hall site we know today. £160 towards the purchase was donated by Lt. Col. Pearson.

Bramcote Memorial Hall Today

Bramcote Memorial Hall has served the community for nearly 90 years. It remained largely unchanged until October 2001 when it was extended (the new extension is on the left of the photograph), with funding from the National Lottery and other sources, to meet the high demand for its facilities.

Acknowledgements

Bramcote History Group is indebted to the families and friends of former residents of Bramcote who are featured in this book. Without their help in answering our questions, searching their family archives and loaning us their treasured memorabilia and pictures, our research would have been both less fun and less satisfying.

We are grateful to all those who have offered their professional expertise and encouragement, including the staff at Nottinghamshire Archives, the University of Nottingham Manuscripts and Special Collections, the Nottingham Local Studies Library, Erewash Museum and the libraries in Beeston, Stapleford, Sandiacre and Toton. Cliff Housley, Regimental Historian of The Sherwood Foresters and Dr. Stuart Wilson have advised on military matters.

Ron Glen and The Memorial Hall Trustees gave their support to this project and allowed us access to their archives which were enhanced by the loan of some photographs from John Barber's collection. David Ottewell and Brian Lund have been generous in allowing us to use some of their pictures from "Stapleford and Bramcote on old picture postcards". Access to Paula Hammond's collection of church magazines, which we were unable to find elsewhere, was invaluable. We also appreciated the help supplied by various people associated with Beeston Boys' Brigade in connection with Stephen Hetley Pearson's records.

We have been granted permission to use some images from "Picture The Past" (www.picturethepast.org.uk) which allows access to historic images from library and museum collections across Derby, Derbyshire, Nottingham and Nottinghamshire.

Those who have helped to research, write, illustrate, compile and edit this volume are Val Bird, Anne Clark, Ann Gray, Janet Martin, Stephen Austin, Jill Ward, Julia Padmore, Lucy Beardsley, Richard and Pauline Henshaw, Edward Motteram, Mike Mountford and Lynda Spencer. In addition to the book, we have also produced an archive of material that can be shared with those who wish to take this research further and rectify any errors!

Sources

Sources for our research have been indicated throughout the text and also on the acknowledgements page but there are some specific items and places of retrieval that should be recorded.

Val Bird has a considerable personal collection of materials relating to Bramcote's history and these together with Bramcote History Group's archives have been utilised in many different ways. Other personal collections from which we have been able to loan items are indicated in the acknowledgements.

Military records, census returns, certificates and newspaper copies have been accessed through websites, the various local studies' departments in Nottinghamshire libraries and the Nottingham County Archives Office. A copy of Harry Bartram's diary, which was published privately, can be located at the University of Nottingham Manuscripts and Special Collections Department. The minutes of Bramcote Parish Council are held at the archives office and copies of the parish magazine that have been quoted from belong to either Paula Hammond or Val Bird.

The research team would be pleased to answer any specific queries and can be contacted through the Bramcote History Group's website: www.bramcotehistory.org.uk